# RESCUE ME!

D0347945

1 9 2583797 6

# RESCUE ME!

## How to successfully re-home a rescue dog

## ALISON SMITH

**COLLINS & BROWN**

First published in the United Kingdom in 2011 by
Collins & Brown
10 Southcombe Street
London W14 0RA

An imprint of Anova Books Company Ltd

Copyright © Collins & Brown 2011

Distributed in the United States and Canada by
Sterling Publishing Co, 387 Park Avenue South, New York, NY 10016-8810, USA

All rights reserved. No part of this publication may be reproduced, stored in a retrieval system, or transmitted in any form or by any means, electronic, mechanical, photocopying, recording or otherwise, without the prior written permission of the copyright holder.

All information is correct at time of going to press.

ISBN 978-1-84340-627-3

A CIP catalogue for this book is available from the British Library.

10  9  8  7  6  5  4  3  2  1

Produced by SP Creative Design
All photography by Gerard Brown with the exception of the following:
Dogs Trust: pages 1 (Brian Young), 8, (Brian Young), 9, 10 (Andy Catterall), 15, 19, 107, 119 (Brian Young). Rolando Ugolini: pages 2, 7, 18, 28, 37, 38, 39, 41, 56, 78, 100, 121, 122
Text by Alison Smith

Acknowledgments
The publishers would like to thank the following for their assistance in producing this book: Dogs Trust Snetterton (Barbara Emons, Katie Hooks and Sarah Brown), Marie Joyce, Lucy Constant, Lindsey Lovatt, Sarah Pengelly, Sue Neal, Adelaide Stewart-Jones and Henry Thomson for appearing in the photographs; and Wolfie Allen, Emma Carley, Jan Parr, Michelle Aland, Audrey Cox and Helen Starkie for kindly allowing us to feature their dogs' stories.

Reproduction by Rival Colour Ltd
Printed by 1010 Printing International Ltd, China

This book can be ordered direct from the publisher at www.anovabooks.com

CONTENTS

**DogsTrust**

# FOREWORD

I know first-hand the wonderful ability that dogs have to lift our spirits, make us laugh, respond to our emotions and generally improve our overall wellbeing. Here at Dogs Trust we are lucky enough to witness the positive and sometimes life-changing influence that our canine companions can have on their new owners. We truly believe that bringing a rescue dog into your home and heart is one of the most rewarding experiences any dog lover can have.

I hope this book inspires and helps you to give a rescue dog a second chance.

Clarissa Baldwin OBE

# DOGS TRUST

Formerly known as the National Canine Defence League, the charity was founded in 1891 to protect dogs from 'torture and ill-usage of every kind'. One hundred and twenty years later, Dogs Trust is now one of the UK's leading charities and continues to pursue its goals with determination. It has a non destruction policy and is working towards the day when all dogs can enjoy a happy life, free from the threat of unnecessary destruction. It cares for over 16,000 dogs a year through a network of 17 Rehoming Centres across the UK and ensures that all dogs are matched to the right owner. Training and behaviour advice are provided throughout the duration of the dog's life if needed.

As suggested by its famous slogan, 'A dog is for life, not just for Christmas®', Dogs Trust is dedicated to tackling the causes of unwanted, abandoned and stray dogs through its Rehoming, Neutering and Microchipping Campaigns. It invests heavily in programmes promoting responsible ownership and believes that education and neutering prevent unwanted and abandoned dogs.

Every year Dogs Trust conducts a survey of UK local authorities to highlight the number of stray dogs and what happens to them. In 1997, there were over 136,000 strays of which 22,000 were destroyed by local authorities. This prompted the charity to launch its Campaigns Programme and by 2010 the figure had dropped to In addition, over 426,209 dogs have been neutered and 240,000 have been microchipped.

Dogs Trust also works with local authorities to promote responsible dog ownership. This policy has led to a significant reduction in the number of stray dogs collected, and how many are destroyed. The charity's Education Programme targets the dog owners of tomorrow. In 2009, Dogs Trust held over 3,000 school workshops and spoke to more than 90,000 young people.

The Outreach Projects assist dogs and their owners who are in need of help, providing a veterinary entitlement card scheme for dogs owned by homeless people, a project helping owners find pet-friendly rented accommodation, and a foster service for dogs owned by women fleeing domestic violence.

Dogs Trust works with policy-makers to ensure the welfare of all dogs, advising Government and other agencies on relevant legislation, including the Animal Welfare Act, and campaigning to stamp out puppy farming, improve the lot of racing Greyhounds, and prevent abusive treatment of dogs across the world. As a registered charity, it receives no government funding and relies solely on the generosity of supporters to carry out its work. Further information can be found on www.dogstrust.org.uk or by calling 0207 837 0006.

# CHAPTER 1
# CHOOSING A RESCUE DOG

There are more abandoned dogs than ever before, and animal shelters and rescue organisations are under constant pressure to find them loving and permanent homes. Canines from all walks of life may become unwanted for many reasons, including cruelty, divorce and bereavement or just the novelty of a new puppy wearing off when the hard work begins. Giving a home to a rescue dog can be challenging, but ultimately it will be the most satisfying and heartwarming decision you will ever make.

# LIFESTYLE FACTORS

If you are considering adopting a dog and giving it a home, there are some factors you ought to think about before going ahead. These involve taking a long, hard look at your lifestyle and circumstances – where you live, how much time you have, whether you work full-time or part-time, how large your house and garden are, and whether you have young children.

## What's best for the dog?

The very best family for a dog to go into (whether it's with one person or a family of eight!) is a household that is aware of what rescuing a dog entails. You need not only to be fully prepared for your new pet but also be able to rehome him with the minimum of fuss and the maximum of love and security.

Many dogs end up in rescue for no other reason than they are no longer wanted, although some may be there due to behavioural problems. No shelter would ever attempt to pair you with a dog of uncertain temperament, but some dogs may be fearful or shy, while others may be very boisterous and noisy. Just as people are all slightly different, so too are dogs, and by making the decision to adopt, you will be guaranteed a friend for life... and one who is extremely loving and grateful to you as well.

Many Greyhounds and Lurchers who end up in rescue make devoted family pets.

## What can you offer?

The key word when rehoming any rescue dog is commitment. Dogs are like children: they need your time and attention; they cost you money; and they need to be fed, watered, walked, exercised and played with throughout their life with you.

### Who's at home?

The ideal home for a rescue dog will be one where there is a family member in the house most of the time. This is especially important if the dog you adopt has been abandoned and may panic if he is left alone for long periods.

Small dogs need lots of attention but make excellent and fun companions.

However, if you can't be there with him 24 hours a day, don't worry too much, as there will be always be a suitable dog who fits in with your lifestyle.

### Will it be expensive?

Dogs need to be provided with food, toys, a collar and lead, and bedding and may also require veterinary treatment. After the initial outlay on equipment, you will have to budget for weekly food and treats, so take this into account.

### The right temperament

If you have young children or other existing pets, be aware that some rescue dogs may not be suitable for you. A good rescue organisation will talk to you about your lifestyle and family, and will try hard to pair you with a dog who will fit in easily with your way of life, with the least upheaval for him.

### Make a list!
List all the useful things to consider. How many hours will the dog be left alone each day? Do you have children? Or other dogs? Do you have a garden? Do you live in a flat, in a city or the countryside? Do you have room for a large dog or a small one? How much exercise can you offer? Would you prefer a quiet dog or a vivacious one? Your answers will help you decide which is the right dog for you.

# THE RIGHT DOG FOR YOU

We all have different lifestyles, and the key to successfully rehoming a dog is to choose one who will be content to fit in with your way of life. Ask yourself what you want from this new relationship. Do you visualise long country walks or a run around the block? Do you like the idea of grooming your dog or would you be happier with a low-maintenance coat? Can you afford to feed a large dog? Do you want a dog who is small and easily carried? Add these wishes to your list and you will begin to get a good idea of what will suit you best.

## Adult or puppy?

The big difference you will find in rescuing a dog, as opposed to looking for a specific pedigree breed or crossbreed, is that there will be more adult and elderly dogs than puppies needing good homes.

Whilst puppies are undeniably cute, there are huge benefits in taking on a slightly older dog. Many adult dogs will come to you fully housetrained, and most will be familiar with walking on a lead, wearing a collar and perhaps even understanding basic obedience commands, such as 'Sit' and 'Stay'. Of course, this is not the case with all dogs – remember that many have ended up in rescue due to insufficient socialisation, communication and contact with their previous owners. However, there are many dogs who are there as a result of families splitting up or their owners becoming ill or dying and being unable to care for them anymore. These dogs tend to be better behaved, as their environment was more normal before being rescued.

If you really want a puppy, you may have to be prepared to wait longer than for an adult dog, as unwanted puppies tend not to end up in rescue until they grow older and develop problems. Sometimes pregnant bitches or mothers and young puppies are abandoned by their owners.

## Elderly dogs

Don't forget that lots of shelters also have elderly dogs looking for a 'forever' home for what remains of their lives. Don't dismiss these older dogs – they are often overlooked in favour of their younger companions, but think how happy and satisfying you could make their last years.

# Girl or boy?

Most shelters nowadays will make sure that both male dogs and bitches are neutered before they are rehomed. This is to prevent even more unwanted puppies in the future. Many people don't believe there is much difference between owning a male or a female, especially if a dog has been castrated, which tends to calm down even the most enthusiastic boys. If you don't have a strong preference for a particular sex, visit your local rescue centre with an open mind. Many people report that they came away with the dog they least expected, and, indeed, in lots of cases it is the dog who chooses you, rather than the other way round! Be prepared to be flexible.

All sorts of dogs end up in rescue, so you must find the right one for you and your lifestyle.

# Big or small? One or two?

Do you want a large or a small dog? A lot depends on how much space you have: a small dog may be happy in a flat or tiny house but a larger dog needs more room and a garden. Small dogs eat less food and tend to live longer.

Do you want one or two dogs? Some rescues may take in a pair from the same home and will recommend that they are rehoused together. If so, could you offer a home to two? If you already have a dog – or other pets – you must inform the staff at the rescue centre and only look for a dog with a good temperament who has been accustomed to living alongside other animals.

# PURE-BRED OR CROSS-BRED?

Most shelters have a mix of pedigree and crossbreed dogs, so it is a good idea to go along with an idea of what sort of dog you would feel happy living with. Many crossbreeds have a discernible mix of different breeds in their genetic makeup, so let's take a look at the different groups of canines and their typical temperaments and behaviour traits.

## Gundogs

This group includes some of the most popular and best-loved dogs, including the Labrador and Golden Retriever as well as all the Spaniels and Pointers.

- Gundogs make lovely, loyal pets. They are intelligent and easy to train, love water and retrieving balls and sticks.
- These dogs need a lot of exercise: a minimum of an hour a day of walking with some free-running thrown in wherever possible.
- Gundogs are great with children and should fit in easily with other animals.

Golden Retrievers are relatively easy to train and make good pets.

## Utility

The Utility group is an eclectic mixture of dogs, and ranges from the beautiful Dalmatian to the blue-tongued Chow Chow and the dainty little Shih Tzu.

- This group's diversity means that the dogs who are included within it differ radically. If you fancy a larger dog, maybe look for a Dalmatian. For a smaller companion, why not try a Lhasa Apso or a Spitz-type, which is more of a lap dog and easy to exercise and maintain?
- Don't forget the Poodles, which come in three sizes: Standard (large), Toy (small) and Miniature (even smaller). They are devoted dogs who love exercise and playing games, and are great with children. There are often lots of Poodle-crosses in rescue centres.

## Terriers

If you want a smaller dog, consider a Terrier or Terrier-cross. In this group are Staffordshire Bull Terriers (see page 19), Jack Russells and Border Terriers, to name but a few.

The Cairn Terrier is a feisty small dog and a good companion.

- Terriers are vivacious dogs, who are rarely still and are always eager to play. They enjoy as much exercise as you can give, love digging up buried treasure, and are particularly good with children.
- If you have other dogs already, discuss this with the staff at the rescue centre, as Terriers can be quite territorial.

## Hounds

This group boasts the elegant Afghan, busy Beagle, and the short-legged, eternally cute, though sometimes stubborn, Dachshund.

- Hounds are known for their speed (sighthounds) and acute sense of smell (scenthounds). Exercise depends on size and build, with larger hounds usually needing more than smaller ones.
- Hounds make wonderful pets, and crossbreeds with a proportion of hound will be a great addition to your family.

Greyhounds are very gentle.

### Greyhounds

The Greyhound is a beautiful dog: graceful, devoted to his owner and requiring very little exercise. He suits almost any lifestyle due to his laid-back attitude. There are dozens of Greyhound rescues, with most dogs coming from a racing background. Sadly, many are considered 'past it' in terms of racing by the age of three or four years and hundreds are put down. The lucky ones are taken in by rescue and offered a good home although many are not well socialised after a life of kennels and racing and may be aloof initially. If you have children, explain to them that they must treat their new pet respectfully until he becomes familiar with them. Once you have gained his trust, he is a fantastic dog to own. He will eat, sleep, eat, go for a walk, sleep, sleep and sleep!

## Working

These are the biggest dogs in the seven
groups, Working dogs love their exercise
and their food. The Rottweiler can be a
fiercely loyal friend, and the Great Dane
is a lovely pet for adults and children.

- Working dogs need plenty of space
  – they are generally quite large dogs
  who will sprawl all over your home.
- They also require a lot of exercise
  and need to be fed the right amount

Rottweilers can make loyal pets.

  of highly nutritious food to keep them in good physical condition.
- As their name suggests, they are born workers and get bored easily if they
  have nothing to do. They like to play and need lots of mental stimulation.

## Pastoral

The Pastoral group includes the breeds with herding instincts, including the
adorable Bearded Collie, the German Shepherd and Border Collie.

- Although they are generally smaller cousins to the Working group, these
  active dogs still require lots of room and exercise in order to reach their
  full potential. If you live in a flat or a small house, you may have difficulty
  in rehoming a Working or Pastoral dog. However, they are ideal for
  people with plenty of energy, large gardens and nearby parks.
- Most breeds in this group usually fit in well with other dogs if they are
  introduced slowly and sensibly. They are also great with children.

## Toys

The tiny Toy breeds are ideal for owners with
less space and time for exercise. This group
includes the Pug, Yorkshire Terrier and Chinese
Crested Dog. Many of these dogs need homes
as they are often bought as fashion accessories
and, consequently, are soon tired of.

- Although most Toy breeds don't need
  masses of exercise, they love daily walks.
  What they won't enjoy is a five-mile hike
  – you will end up carrying them!

Pugs are fun-loving and feisty.

- They fit well into most families and often become the 'boss' of other dogs in the household, even if they are considerably larger.
- Long-haired breeds, such as the Pekingese and Yorkshire Terrier, need to be groomed and bathed regularly to keep their coats clean and tidy.

## Crossbreeds

Full of hybrid vigour and usually bursting to please, one of the best dogs that you could ever own is a crossbreed, due to the variety of breeds that have gone into creating him.

- Crossbreeds come in all shapes and sizes with equally different temperaments and personalities. Whether you want a laid-back giant or a small bundle of energy, you'll find the perfect companion at a rescue centre.
- They are usually very healthy, rarely need a vet and have lovely temperaments. They are just as important an addition to a family as a pedigree dog, and they are equally loving, intelligent and loyal.

Staffordshire Bull Terriers are very affectionate dogs.

### Staffordshire Bull Terriers and bull breeds

Unfortunately, the Stafford is one of the most maligned of all dogs. This loving, fearless and handsome dog has received some terrible press, but a well-reared and socialised Stafford is actually known as the 'Nanny Dog' because of his love of children and devotion to them. Many Staffords end up in rescue, some the victims of the so-called Ego Dog fashion, where young gang members use them as weapons. Pure-bred and Stafford-crosses are very popular with families who are looking for a rescue dog. These dogs enjoy lots of exercise, a healthy diet and plenty of mental stimulation to prevent boredom. Some Staffords do not like being left alone for long periods and may be noisy until their owner returns.

Like the Stafford, there are other Bull breeds that have had a worse press than they deserve. The Bullmastiff, Bulldog and Mastiff are sometimes labelled as dangerous but this is not necessarily true. These dogs can easily fall into the wrong hands and are blamed for attacks on people and children, but they can make wonderful pets when they are well-socialised and treated with kindness – even a Yorkshire Terrier will become aggressive in the wrong hands! If you are considering rehoming a bull breed, ask the rescue centre staff for their advice – they are always happy to help.

# So You Want To Adopt?

If you think that taking on a rescue dog is right for you, the next decision you will need to make is where to go to find one that fits your personal preferences, lifestyle and circumstances.

## Rescue centres

In the UK, the two main general rescue organisations are the Dogs Trust and RSPCA. Both are looking constantly to rehome many hundreds of dogs each month. Crossbreeds and pedigrees come through their doors, ranging from

---

**Pedigree versus mongrel**

A dog will enhance your life, no matter what breed, size, age or shape. The pros and cons in the crossbreed-pedigree debate are listed below.

**Pedigree pros**

- Pedigree breeds have a uniformity of size, coat and, sometimes, temperament.
- Health problems may be predictable.
- Support can be gained through the breed network.
- Even from rescue, the dog's family history may be available.
- There may be the opportunity to show your dog in competitions.

**Pedigree cons**

- Your puppy or dog will be more expensive to buy.
- You may have to wait months for availability.
- Your pet may be targeted by thieves.
- Some pedigrees are prone to hereditary health problems.

**Crossbreed pros**

- Each crossbreed looks unique.
- They often enjoy good health – better than many pedigree dogs.
- They cost less to buy.
- They are readily available.
- They are cheaper to insure.
- They are less likely to be stolen.

**Crossbreed cons**

- They may look cute as puppies but not necessarily as fully-grown adults.
- Their temperament may be uncertain and cannot be predicted.
- They may be excluded from showing or agility competitions.
- They may not be fully vaccinated.

---

puppies to elderly dogs. There are other dog charities as well, some run by individuals from home whereas others are on a larger scale, but in all cases these dogs are looking for a good home as quickly as possible.

## Breed rescues

As well as rehoming centres there are also hundreds of breed rescue societies. These charities rescue pedigree dogs who are unwanted,

When you arrive, ask the rescue centre staff any questions you may have.

have been overbred or have become homeless due to divorce, moving home or illness. If you are on the lookout for a pedigree dog, contact your local breed rescue. As with any other rescue, you may have to take on an older dog as puppies are rare and tend to go quickly. Breed rescue co-ordinators will talk to you at length to make sure you can offer the dog a good home and will also be there to answer your questions. Use this time to interact with the dogs. A home visit will usually be required if you wish to adopt.

Take your time to look at the dogs, assessing their behaviour and response to you.

# AT THE CENTRE

Now that you've had a look at all the different options you are ready to begin the process of adopting a dog and giving him a new, loving home. The next step is to find a shelter in your area, so you can arrange a visit, talk to the staff about what you can offer and take a look at the available dogs.

## Rehoming centres

If your mind is still open to what type of dog you want, try to visit a rehoming centre first. Most centres are open daily, so make a quick telephone call to check the opening hours and visiting times before setting out. You will be greeted by well-trained staff who will chat to you about what sort of dog you are looking for. Use this time to ask them any questions you may have.

### Questionnaire

At the centre you will be asked to fill in a questionnaire about you, your lifestyle and the kind of dog you would like. This will help the staff to offer you a suitable rescue dog – one who will fit easily into his new home. Always be honest when you answer the questions: remember that this is not a test you have to pass.

You will be interviewed by the rescue centre staff who will ask you about your circumstances.

### Have a look around

View the different types of dog up close and get an idea of what you like. Remember that all the dogs may well look adorable, but you need to find a suitable one. There's no need to choose the first dog you see, and you can visit the centre on more than one occasion before rushing into a decision without due consideration. The staff may recommend which dogs they think are right for you and will give you the opportunity to spend some time with the dog in a secure environment or take him for a walk to get to know each other better.

### Home visits

Once your questionnaire has been filled in, you have had a look around and found a potential dog, your home will be visited by a member of the rescue staff. Again, this is not a test. The centre needs to check that you can offer a dog a safe environment. If they have any concerns they will discuss them with you and recommend any changes that may be needed.

## Breed rescues

If you decide a pedigree dog is the right choice for you and the local rescue centres do not have the breed you want, you need to find a breed rescue in your area. Breed rescues will not have many dogs on offer but, depending on the breed, you may be matched up with a suitable dog within a few weeks.

### What can you offer?

Like an all-breed shelter, a breed rescue will want to ask you all sorts of questions about you, your family, your working hours and lifestyle. Again, this is not a judgement on you: all these dogs have already suffered the loss of a home and the rescue staff are just making sure they won't have to go through the trauma and upheaval again. A home visit will also be arranged should you decide to go ahead with adopting a pedigree dog.

You can assess whether a dog is right for you by taking him for a walk on the lead and playing together.

# CHOOSING YOUR DOG

The checks have been done and you may well have visited your chosen rescue a couple of times; now you want to find a dog to take home with you. For many people, this can be difficult as all the dogs are appealing in different ways, and it's especially hard to overlook puppies.

## What to look for

By now you will have a good idea of the type of dog that will suit you best, and the rescue staff will have offered advice and guidance as to which dogs are right for you. Try to narrow your choices down to the dogs who are the desired size and age with the right coat and temperament. You could try making a shortlist of the ones that appeal to you.

The rescue centre staff will give you and the dog time to get to know each other better.

## Health concerns

Some dogs, especially pedigrees, can sometimes be affected by hereditary diseases – illnesses that may be specific to a particular breed. If you are worried about this, do ask the staff for more information at the time of your interview.

**Checklist**
- Is the dog the right size?
- Does he appear healthy? Look for a shiny, wet nose, healthy-looking coat, and an alert and friendly disposition.
- Have you spent time with him and perhaps taken him for a walk?
- Have you checked that he is neutered and microchipped?
- Is your home ready and have you made any necessary changes?
- Have you registered with a local vet and taken out pet insurance?

## Meet and greet

Many centres will encourage you to spend time with a few of the dogs on your shortlist. Ask if you can take the dog out for a short walk around the grounds – if you are unsure, ask a member of staff to come with you. Spend time talking to the dog and making a fuss of him. This will give you an idea of his temperament and whether you feel comfortable with each other. Introduce him to your family (especially if you have young children). This will allow you to watch how they interact with each other. Always make sure that the children are supervised and don't let them get over-excited at the first meeting.

Get to know the dog you like – make several visits if necessary until you're sure that he's right for you.

## Cost

Once you have chosen your new dog, you will be asked for a donation to the rescue. This may seem quite expensive but it is used to pay for the veterinary and health costs incurred by the centre and to help it continue its work. Most,

if not all, rescue dogs will have been neutered (they will be unable to sire or give birth to puppies) and microchipped for easy identification should they become lost. A microchip is a small, harmless chip that is usually inserted at the base of the dog's neck. It can be scanned easily and will contain your dog's details.

Take the dog for a walk, spend time with him and play some games.

# CASE STUDY

## JACK

Jack, an Akita-Staffordshire Bull Terrier cross, was a long-term resident at the Dogs Trust centre in Leeds before he was adopted by Emma Carley and her partner Jamie. The rescue staff were were delighted when he was rehomed. Emma had never owned a dog before but had enjoyed helping look after her mother's Spaniel. When he died, she went along to her local Dogs Trust in order to volunteer as a dog walker and spotted Jack in the first kennel.

'My heart melted when I first saw him – he looked so sad and had even stopped eating as he'd been there for 16 months and was depressed. The Dogs Trust had tried radio and television appeals but no-one wanted him. I went home and told Jamie, and the moment he saw Jack he said, "He's coming home with us" and the rest is history. Jack settled in right away with no problems at all – like many middle-aged dogs in rescue, he was house trained and well behaved.

'He immediately became part of our family and we couldn't understand why

| | |
|---|---|
| **Age** | 9 years old |
| **Breed** | Crossbreed |
| **Size** | Medium |
| **Colour** | Brindle and white |
| **Adopted** | Emma and Jamie |

he'd been at the centre so long. He's so soft and loves cuddles. However, he needs a lot of attention and we can't leave him on his own for long. I work during the day and Jamie works nights, so there's always someone home with him 24/7. Jamie has an energetic playtime with him every morning before they both settle down for a sleep. Then it's a more sedate playtime and cuddles when I get home. We spend every weekend together the three of us as a family. We have to be careful where we walk him as Jack doesn't like other dogs. We don't know the reason for this but it isn't a problem for us and we just make sure that we keep him well away from any potentially difficult situations.

'We can't imagine life without Jack now – we adore him and think he's just perfect!'

'Jack is great company and gives us so much love. I never thought I'd end up with a dog with his mixed breed heritage but you can't judge a book by its cover.'

# CHAPTER 2

# BRINGING YOUR NEW DOG HOME

This is going to be a very special day for you and your dog. Even if you feel apprehensive, there's no need to worry. Dogs are extremely adaptable and, with patience and love, your efforts will be rewarded. If you work, take a few days' holiday while your dog settles in, and sort out with your family who's going to be responsible for walking him, feeding him and taking him to the vet. If it's you who ends up walking him on a cold, wet night, just smile and remember that pet parenting is a privilege, not a chore.

# GETTING READY

Be prepared and establish the boundaries before your new friend arrives in your home. Think about putting a dog bed in every room where you and your family will be spending time with your dog. Dog beds represent sensible and comfortable alternatives to letting him jump on the furniture. Close the doors to rooms that are off limits and use child gates for blocking off areas with no doors, like hallways and staircases.

## Insurance

Many people choose to take out insurance for their dog. Pet insurance will cover any veterinary treatment that may become necessary during his lifetime. There are dozens of companies offering a wide range of policies, so shop around and compare what's on offer to find one that suits your requirements as well as your pocket. Premiums are relatively inexpensive but be sure to read the small print carefully before signing up to ensure comprehensive cover. If in doubt, seek advice from your vet or the staff at the rescue centre.

**Equipment checklist**
You will need to buy the following before your dog comes home:
- Two dog bowls – one for food and one for water.
- Food – check with the rescue centre which food he usually eats.
- A lead and collar – the collar should fit your dog snugly without being too loose or too tight and you should be able to get two fingers under it.
- At least one dog bed and some soft, cosy bedding.
- A crate (optional) – a metal cage which many dogs like as a 'haven'.
- Grooming brushes and combs, especially for longer-coated breeds.
- Dog treats – optional but nice and perfect for rewarding good behaviour.
- Worming tablets.
- Flea products.
- Toys – make sure they are safe and the right size for your new dog.

Every dog needs a comfortable bed in a quiet place away from people and noise.

# SAFETY FIRST

Your home visit from a member of staff at the rescue centre may have highlighted any causes for concern with regard to safety in your house and garden. It is very important that your dog is secure and not exposed to harm. Remember that he may well be nervous initially and everything will be new to him. This is the time when you must be vigilant and stay with him when he's in the garden to make sure he cannot escape.

## Garden safety

Do ensure that all the fences are solid and intact with no loose or broken boards and that all garden doors and gates are dog-proof – a small dog can quite easily crawl under a gate with a gap of 12–15cm (5–6in), so attach some wire netting at ground level. Check grassy areas for anything your dog could pick up and swallow, such as old pegs, small stones or children's toys.

The rescue staff will microchip your dog, so it's easier to find him if he gets lost.

If you have a garden shed, keep it securely locked with all weedkillers and pesticides out of the dog's way on a high shelf. Also, be aware of any poisonous plants in your garden, such as yew, rhododendrons, holly and mistletoe berries, spring bulbs, foxgloves and some fungi. Keep your dog well away from them.

## Dog-proof your home

Some dogs, especially puppies, love to chew, so you must make sure that all electrical wires are well out of reach. Put any household cleaners and chemicals up high or store in a locked or bolted cupboard, as you would for a toddler. Raise all mini-blind and curtain pulls off the floor, so your dog can't get entangled in them or pull them down. Check that

everyone's shoes and slippers are safely put away – a puppy will chew an expensive pair of trainers quite happily. Some people find that it helps to get down on the floor themselves to get a dog's-eye view of every room to see what might tempt a curious canine.

You can fit a child gate at the bottom of the stairs to prevent your dog going up and perhaps falling down. Switch off live electric sockets at floor level, check for any trailing wires and put away the children's toys. Your home should now be dog-proof..

**Keep any electrical appliances well out of your dog's reach.**

**In or out?**
If you want to keep a dog in a heated outdoor kennel, speak to the rescue staff before buying one. Kennels are not suitable for many rehomed dogs who will prefer the security and comfort of living with their new family in a house. You are offering a dog a loving home with you – not a kennel!

# COMING HOME

Today's the day when your new dog is ready to come home and join you and your family. There is an old saying that you never get a second chance to make a first impression, and this is applicable to puppies and dogs, too. No matter how happy you are to bring your dog home and how much you want to make up for the shabby way he was treated in the past, you need to start off right from the very beginning.

## House rules

Decide what the house rules are and stick to them – for at least the first couple of months. Dogs like routine and you must let your new dog know that even though you're the nicest person on earth and the best human he could ever hope to find, your house does have rules and he must follow them.

## At the rescue centre

The staff at the rescue centre will have your dog ready for you on your arrival, and this is the time to ask any last-minute questions, such as when is he usually fed and exercised, and is he accustomed to travelling by car. The ideal time to pick up your new dog is in the morning but it will depend on the rescue centre and their usual arrangements. However, if you can arrange a morning collection, you will have the rest of the day to settle him down and spend some quality time together.

It's a special moment when you leave the rescue centre with your dog for the first time – be patient if he is nervous.

## Transport

If you are picking up your dog in a car, it's a good idea to ask a friend or family member to accompany you. You can buy doggy 'seatbelts', which are easy to fit, but bear in mind that he may not have been in a car before, so take a soft towel or blanket and let him travel home on the back seat with someone sitting beside him, stroking him and talking quietly and soothingly.

If you are collecting a puppy, it may even be possible to carry him home inside a coat or blanket. Again, you will have to reassure him all the time as he may be nervous at first.

## Crates

Older dogs may be happy to travel home in a crate in the back of your car. This is a safe way to travel, but do make sure that the dog is calm and appears happy with the situation. On no account allow a new dog to be moving around freely inside a car – accidents can easily happen this way.

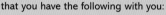

**Checklist**

The day you collect your dog, make sure that you have the following with you:

- A towel or blanket (some dogs find it comforting if the bedding has your scent imprinted on it).
- A lead and collar (these may be provided by some rescue centres but check first).
- Tissues and carrier bags (in case of any emergencies).
- A human travelling companion.

If you don't have a companion, make your dog safe and comfortable in the car.

# SETTLING IN A PUPPY

If you're adopting a puppy, be prepared for some disruption and mess. Don't worry about tidying the house; it can soon be put straight. These first days and weeks spent settling in to your new home will be the most important time for both of you, and getting it right now will pay dividends later on.

## First things first

The first thing your puppy will want to do when he gets 'home' is to eat some food and relieve himself. Put him on a soft puppy collar and lead and walk him into the garden, so he can sniff the grass or any area that takes his fancy. Pick a special place and encourage him to 'go' there. Be patient – it may take 10 or 15 minutes before he does what you want him to do. Always praise him warmly when he relieves himself in an approved spot.

## Hello house

Now go into the house and show your puppy round, keeping him on the lead at first. If he lifts his leg, tell him 'No' and then take him outside immediately. Offer him a treat for relieving himself in the right place – this will reinforce the message and he will soon learn to go to the toilet outside. Remember that he will be excited and anxious about his new home, so don't be surprised if he has bouts of panting and pacing, housetraining accidents, excessive drinking or chewing, or even a tummy upset. Tell your family to resist the temptation to overwhelm him. Give him some time and space to get settled and try to avoid getting him over-excited. At this point, you may want to feed him.

**Your new puppy will need:**
- To be fed three to four times a day if he is under six months old.
- Supervised playtimes and exercise – but not too much initially.
- As much rest and sleep as he wants.
- Encouragement to spend short periods of time alone.
- To be slowly socialised around other animals, adult dogs and humans.
- To be registered with a vet.
- To become used to being handled and groomed gently.

# Housetraining your puppy

It's easy to housetrain dogs of all ages, especially puppies. Get your puppy trained to go outside for his toilet right from the beginning. If you start this routine straight away, he will soon get the message. A puppy's instinct is to relieve himself upon waking and after eating, so make sure he goes out as soon as he wakes up and after every meal and drink. Stay with him, even if it's cold or wet, and encourage him, praising him when he does anything.

### Using newspaper

Newspaper training is an alternative to going outside. Choose an area and lay some sheets of newspaper down for your puppy. The best location is near the door he will eventually exit to do his business. Keep moving it closer and put

the puppy on the paper when he eats, drinks or wakes up. He'll soon learn to relieve himself there. This is useful if you live in a flat or he is shut up all night. At some point, you can dispense with the newspaper and let him out.

**Always go outside with your puppy and stay with him.**

# LOOKING AFTER A PUPPY

Puppies are the biggest time-wasters you will ever meet. You will end up watching their antics for hours on end and then wonder where the day went. There is lots to do with a puppy, however, so at least you can waste time constructively.

## Feeding times

Puppies up to the age of six to eight months thrive best on a few smaller meals per day rather than one or two larger ones. Aim for three to four meals of your chosen food. Try to give your dog breakfast, lunch, dinner and supper, and don't forget to put him out to relieve himself after each meal. Always have fresh water available.

Give your puppy small meals several times a day – less as he gets older.

## Playtime

Puppies love to play and it's also a good way to keep them mentally stimulated. You can buy toys for your puppy, but he will be happy to play on the floor with you. Everything is new to him, so a game of chase with your hands is just as exciting as an expensive toy. Do not try to engage him in rough-and-tumble games that could hurt him or encourage aggression.

**Toys**

We all like to buy toys for our new dogs. If you want to treat yours, go to a good pet shop, but remember that expensive is not always best.

- Buy toys that are the right size – bigger dogs need bigger toys than smaller ones.
- Check the toys for small parts, as these can be removed and swallowed by a puppy.
- All dogs love to play at catching bubbles and you can even buy meat-flavoured ones from many pet stores.
- Look for a safe cuddly toy, which your puppy may like to sleep with.
- Avoid squeaky toys initially, as the small squeaks are easy to swallow.

## Lead training

Start by putting a collar on your puppy for a few hours at a time until he gets accustomed to it. Don't worry if he tries to 'scratch' it off; this is normal and he's doing it because it feels strange. Getting him used to a lead takes time and patience. Never drag him along on his lead as this will cause more problems than it will solve. Use praise each time he walks and encourage him all the time.

## Exercise

Exercise for the first few months of a puppy's life should always be gentle and gradual. A run round the house and garden will often be sufficient for a smaller dog whereas short walks and a run around the garden are enough for a larger dog. Young dogs tire easily, so don't expect too much of them.

## Grooming and coat care

Establish a routine of grooming your puppy and checking his nails, teeth and ears. This will ensure you pick up on any health problems and will also help you to bond with each other. Many dogs find this time very relaxing... you will, too.

## Chewing

Puppies lose their baby teeth at around seven months. Like children, they like to chew on things to alleviate any discomfort, so provide your dog with some appropriate chews to prevent him attacking your shoes and the table legs.

## Vaccinations

Make an appointment as soon as you can to see your local vet. Even if your puppy has already had some of his vaccinations, a health check is still a good idea. Remember to take along with you any paperwork relating to his veterinary care to date. Your vet will give him a health check.

**Puppies love to chew, so give them hard-wearing toys.**

# SOCIALISING A PUPPY

Early socialisation is the most important thing that you and your puppy can do together in the first few months. He will come to you with very few social skills and it is your job to turn him into a loving, caring confident and obedient friend.

## Meeting people

One of the most important things your puppy can learn is to be comfortable around all sorts of people. Introduce people as often as possible, starting with family members and progressing to neighbours, friends and tradesmen. Ask visitors to put their hands out slowly and allow him to sniff at them, at which point they can make a fuss of him. Don't let him get too excited or over-exuberant. He needs to know that he cannot jump up at people.

## Other dogs

Do not allow your new puppy to play with adolescent dogs until he has been socialised. Source some other puppies as playmates and match them closely in age – for example, don't put your 10-week-old puppy with a 16-week-old one. Try to find playmates with a similar temperament – if you have a quiet, timid toy breed, don't match him with an older, exuberant Labrador.

## Training and socialisation classes

Puppy and adult training classes play a valuable role in socialisation. Here your puppy will be able to interact with other people and dogs in a safe environment. Puppy classes allow your dog to develop good canine social manners while playing with other puppies in a non-threatening and controlled setting. Shy and fearful puppies will quickly gain confidence, whereas rough bullies learn to tone down their behaviour and be more gentle.

## Outside…

Never take your dog's temperament for granted. The great outdoors can be a frightening place for a youngster, and there may be the occasional scary surprise. Treating your dog on walks will help him form positive associations with people, other dogs and traffic. Offer him a tasty treat every time a car, big truck or noisy motorcycle goes by. Treat him whenever another dog or person passes. Praise him and offer a treat whenever he greets another dog or person in a friendly fashion, and also when a child approaches.

## ...and inside

Hoovers, fireworks, loud bangs, and noisy and boisterous children can all cause stress and fright in a young dog. Try to introduce him to things one at a time. Use a reassuring voice while you turn on the vacuum cleaner or hairdryer; and let him sit on your knee when the children play in the same room. Get him used to being around when you are doing your daily chores.

You should get your puppy accustomed to meeting as many people as possible.

# SETTLING IN AN ADULT DOG

Adult dogs tend to be calmer and more relaxed than puppies. They may already have an established routine and will have developed their own distinct personality. In most cases, an adult dog will be fully housetrained when he comes to you and will understand basic commands. Although some degree of retraining may be necessary as he gets used to his new surroundings, usually the hard work has already been done.

## Behaviour

The rescue centre may have given you an accurate assessment of your dog's character, which has been gleaned from information from previous owners and/or their own internal assessment programme. As social animals, dogs may need time – sometimes several months – to adjust to their new social group before showing their true behaviour and temperament. You need to be patient and wait for your dog to settle in and adjust to his new life with you.

## His own place

Changing homes can be a traumatic experience for adult dogs (although many are extremely adaptable). They may have lost 'friends' and familiar surroundings, so it's your job to make sure you have prepared a safe and

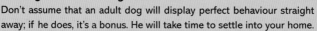

**Settling in an adult dog**
Don't assume that an adult dog will display perfect behaviour straight away; if he does, it's a bonus. He will take time to settle into your home.
- An adult dog can be vulnerable and inconsistent.
- An adult with little or no training should be treated in the same way as a puppy, so always start with the basics of housetraining and obedience commands.
- Even a fully housetrained adult dog may have the odd 'accident' in the house during the settling-in period – be patient and understanding.
- It's best if the house rules don't keep changing. Establish them kindly but consistently from day one and don't allow bad or unwanted behaviour 'just for now'.
- Go easy on the cuddles until you are really accustomed to each other.
- If you have children or other dogs, take things slowly when it comes to introductions.

**Be sensitive when introducing your new rescue dog to an established family dog.**

happy environment for your dog. Make sure you provide a quiet sleeping area where the new arrival can feel safe, equipped with a cosy blanket or cushion, as well as some water and a food bowl. This provides a 'time out' place to which your dog can escape for some peaceful rest.

## Introductions

If you're introducing an adopted dog to another adult dog, don't assume that they will get along immediately. Let them get to know each other gradually, always giving the resident dog plenty of attention, so the new companion is not seen as a threat. And bear in mind that dogs that have not been spayed or neutered are more prone to fighting. With a resident cat, the road to social harmony often takes a little longer for adult dogs, but it is achievable in most circumstances. Do remember that sighthounds, such as Greyhounds and Lurchers, have an inbuilt instinct to chase other creatures, so introducing these dogs to a cat may take a little more time and patience.

## Routine

Routine is the best thing you can offer your adult dog. It is a great cure for anxiety and a dog with a routine is a happy dog: he knows what is going to come next. A good routine will be made up of regular feeding times, regular exercise and walks, a good amount of play and mental stimulation, and a regular bedtime. Create a routine that works for both you and your dog.

# LOOKING AFTER YOUR DOG

An adult dog may come with a great deal of training, or with very little. Be guided by the rescue centre on how to proceed, but you may have to put in extra time and effort to teach your old dog new tricks. As with puppies, take things slowly and don't expect miracles. Start with basic commands, such as 'Sit' and use lots of praise and treats to reward correct behaviour.

## Feeding

Always feed your dog at around the same time each day, as this will establish a good routine. To ease the transition to his new home, stick with the same food he was fed before his arrival – it's just one less new thing for him to cope with. If you decide to change brands, make the transition as smooth as possible, as dogs can often be sensitive to dietary changes. Start by mixing the new food with the previous brand, gradually increasing the proportion

Get down on the floor at your dog's level and have fun playing games with him.

over one week to 10 days, until your dog is only eating the new food. Don't be surprised if he has an upset tummy initially – this is quite normal.

## Exercise

You also need to establish a routine for exercising your dog. If he will walk beside you on a lead and is used to traffic, vary his walks as much as possible. Roadwork is good for building muscle and keeping his nails short, but take him to local parks or the countryside, too. Do not let him off the lead until you have good recall (he comes back to you when called). Wherever you go, take something to clean up after him – nappy bags are ideal.

**Mind games**
Mental stimulation is very important to all dogs, whatever their personality or energy level. Spend at least 15 minutes every day playing with a favourite toy together, or use treats to encourage your dog to chase round the garden and play hide and seek. This time together will pay dividends as you form a closer bond.

## Grooming

All dogs need grooming, even short-coated ones. However, while a wiry Jack Russell Terrier may just need a quick brush once or twice a week, a long-haired Afghan Hound or Yorkshire Terrier may require daily grooming.

**Short-coated dogs**
These dogs need very little grooming at all. Most dogs moult (lose hairs) at some time or another, so give them a brush every week. Poodles have non-shedding coats, making them the ideal choice for anyone with an allergy.

**Long-coated dogs**
Dogs with long, glossy coats can be hard work, and you will need to spend some time each day brushing your dog's coat, first with a bristle brush and then with a comb. Tease out any tangles and matted hair gently. As the coat gets longer, or if it needs stripping or clipping, consider visiting a grooming parlour. You can ask them to show you how to do it yourself, if you like.

**Harsh-coated dogs**
Terriers, Lurchers and some Dachshunds have coats that feel almost wiry to the touch. Wire coats do need grooming to maintain them and you should use a slicker brush for the best results. Visit a grooming professional to have your dog's coat stripped (all the dead hair removed) at least twice a year.

# CASE STUDY

# SIERRA

Michelle wanted to rescue a Shih Tzu as a companion for her older dog Ruby when she registered on the Dogs Trust website. She didn't have to wait too long at all before the Bridgend Shelter contacted her regarding Sierra, who had been abused and abandoned by a puppy farm and was found scavenging. Michelle, who lives in London, made three trips to South Wales to get to know Sierra before bringing her home.

'I took Ruby with me but initially she ignored Sierra, who was very timid. Because she had never been socialized she was frightened of everything, but I persevered and the rescue staff said it would be beneficial for her to have an older dog as a role model. When I eventually brought her home, she followed Ruby's example in everything and used her as a guide to how she should behave and react to different people, dogs, environments and situations.

'Although Sierra needed only minimal training, I had to proceed very slowly with her and only introduced her to people gradually. Because she had always been confined, she wasn't used to having any freedom. Her first walk along the

| | |
|---|---|
| **Age** | 3 years old |
| **Breed** | Shih Tzu |
| **Size** | Small |
| **Colour** | Fawn |
| **Adopted** | Michelle |

street and around the block was terrifying for her but she soon grew more confident and started to follow Ruby's lead and tune into her moods. She's been with me four months now and is walking much further, she's put on weight and filled out, and her coat is much healthier.

'I had originally wanted a male dog, not a female, but it's worked out brilliantly – much better than I expected – and has been a win-win for all of us because Sierra has not only settled in well but has also energised Ruby. I believe that our success is down to the expertise of the Dogs Trust staff in matching rescue dogs with potential owners. I would advise anyone looking for a dog to always allow their trainers to guide you on what 's right for you – it may not be what you think! Sierra is such a lovely dog and she just loves sitting on my lap. I couldn't imagine life without her now.'

> '**It's been a win-win for all of us because Sierra has not only settled in so well but has also energised my older dog and has given her a new lease of life.**'

# CHAPTER 3

# BONDING WITH YOUR NEW DOG

As well as food and exercise, your new dog needs to form a bond with you and your family. For a really good relationship, this bond has to be strong, and it has very little to do with your dog's age or breed. Once this bond is in place between you, nothing can break it, and you will have a loyal and affectionate companion for life.

# COMMUNICATING WITH YOUR DOG

Talking to your dog is one of the most important and basic forms of communication you can have with him and it's not a sign of madness. In fact, you should talk to him as much as you can to get him accustomed to the sound of your voice. Even if you tell him what you are doing, such as 'I'm preparing your dinner now', try to use your voice as much as possible.

## Vocal communication

Words that are repeated often become a second language to dogs. Although they cannot speak our language, like a human baby, they can pick up a lot of words that are repeated consistently. However, unlike a child, they are unlikely to develop a sophisticated understanding of grammar or to think in words, even though some owners claim their dog understands everything they say.

## Word association

What this means is that your dog might be able to make the association between specific words and understand what you mean, once you have established a clear meaning for each of those words. Let's say that your dog has learned to 'fetch' a 'ball' or 'come' for 'dinner', or 'go' for 'walkies'. With patience you can probably communicate with your dog to string those behaviours together. A dog who has learned to fetch an object and bring it to you could be directed instead to go get the ball and carry it to Sally.

Your dog will not understand words for things or actions that are outside his own experiences. We understand only a fraction of what our dogs know about their world. We can only guess at their ability to read body language, see in the dark, hear sounds outside the range that we can hear, and detect scents.

> **More routine**
> Try to be consistent in the things you say to your dog and the way in which you use your body to back this up. He will learn to read your body language quickly before he even starts to recognise the specific words you are using.

Talk to your dog and get to know his body language to aid the bonding process.

# WHAT IS HE SAYING?

Learning how to read your dog's body language will take time and observation. Try to spend just a few minutes every day observing his actions (and reactions) to certain objects, people, other animals and activities. Watch the different body parts (his ears, tails, eyes, lips, hair and overall posture) separately, and see if you can predict which body stances lead to which behaviours or outcomes. By learning to read the tell-tale signs, you will be able to gain a better understanding of your dog.

## Fear

A frightened dog will generally adopt a low stance with his tail tucked in underneath him. He may turn his head away from you and even show the whites of his eyes, and he might also bark.

Some dogs are naturally dominant or submissive, as shown by their body language.

## Confidence

Dogs display confidence in a similar way, regardless of their breed or age. A happy and confident dog will hold his tail up proudly and will generally look alert in his expression, with a relaxed body stance.

## Happy

A happy dog will show the same signs as a confident dog but, in addition, he will usually wag his tail and sometimes hold his mouth open more or even pant mildly. He will appear to be even more friendly and content than the confident dog, with no visible signs of anxiety.

## Playful

A playful dog is happy and excited. His ears are up, his eyes are bright, and his tail wags rapidly. He may jump and run around. He will often exhibit the 'play bow' with his front legs stretched forward, head straight ahead, and rear end up in the air and possibly wiggling. This is an invitation to play!

## Dominant

A dominant dog will try to assert himself over other dogs and sometimes people, too. He will stand tall and confident and may lean slightly forwards. His eyes may be wide and he will make direct eye contact with the other dog or person. If the behaviour is directed at a dog that submits, there is little concern. However, if the other dog also tries to be dominant, a fight may break out. A dog that directs dominant behaviour towards people can pose a serious threat. Do not make eye contact and slowly try to leave. If your dog exhibits this behaviour towards people, professional help may be required.

**Observe your dog**

- Watch your dog over a few days, observing his behaviour and making a note of the way his body reacts to a range of things, such as feeding time, going out, play time and treat time.
- Watch how he interacts with you and other people. Is there a difference?
- Never try to dominate or shout at a dog displaying dominant or aggressive behaviour. If in doubt, call the rescue centre and seek advice.
- Never praise a dog for aggressive or dominant behaviour, and this includes using reassuring language; he will take this as an endorsement from you.

# HOW TO HAVE A HAPPY DOG

Dogs, like children, are happiest when they understand the rules and boundaries that are set for them by their owners, the people who are responsible for their safety and welfare. Dogs do not like ambiguity, and even the most creative breeds still want to know the limits within which they can have their fun. To make a dog happy and confident, we must provide them with meaningful, fair, consistent and appropriately timed and measured feedback about their behaviour. In other words, we need to interact with our dogs.

## Home comforts

Dogs are very social animals and thrive as part of a pack. For your dog, you and your family are his 'pack', and your home is his. Living in a warm and safe environment is really beneficial for his general health and happiness. A dog who is left out all day in the backyard or garden will have no mental stimulation and no human affection, so it stands to reason that he will most certainly not gain happiness and confidence from this situation.

## Give him space

All dogs need their own space for sleeping as well as for seeking refuge when things get too much for them. It's important to provide a bed for your dog. Make sure it is positioned well away from the hustle and bustle of the household, somewhere safe where he can sleep and be quiet.

## Boundaries

This may sound silly, but the more boundaries and rules you set for your dog, the happier and more confident he will become. You have taken over as his pack leader, and if you act in a confident and assertive (but not too

Make your dog sit and wait when you get his lead to take him out for a walk.

Playing with your dog on the floor at his level will be enjoyable for both of you.

dominant) manner, he will quickly pick up on those feelings and messages. Set the guidelines quickly, such as eating times (make him wait), exercise times (when you want them) and quiet times (when you tell him).

## Get on your knees

Get down on the floor at your dog's level a few times a day and play with him, or just have a bit of a love-in by offering loads of pats, belly rubs and hugs. Put your eyes below his and gaze up at him, but be prepared for a few licks.

## Don't shout

Never raise your voice to – or hit – your dog – both are always counter-productive. No matter how big or small he is, he could certainly hurt you but he chooses not to. Respect your dog and he will respect you – he will be less likely to have common behaviour problems and will be a joy to own.

## Be patient

Building up a timid rescue dog's confidence around you, your family and friends can sometimes take weeks or even months. You need to be patient and calm and use quiet encouragement to resolve his anxieties. Your dog might never turn into a bouncing barrel of enthusiasm, but eventually he will learn to feel more comfortable in his own fur.

# BUILDING A LASTING BOND

Expecting an instant bond with your rescue dog – whether he's a puppy or an adult – is a big mistake. Bonding takes time and effort on both sides but, once made, that bond will last for life.

## Time together

Spend some time together on a one-to-one basis, whether it's travelling by car, walking in the park or through busy streets, meeting other people and their dogs, or going to busy events or training classes. Go anywhere that will expose your dog to some unusual situations in which he will automatically look to you for guidance and security. Just by doing this, a bond will start to form.

## Have fun

Make bonding fun for both you and your dog; it doesn't always have to be serious and profound. Try playing with a Frisbee, dancing to music, running round an agility course, or get some popcorn and a few dog treats and curl up on the sofa to watch a movie together. Every year in the United Kingdom there is a 'Take Your Dog to Work Day', so take yours with you.

## Go for a ride

Going out in the car does not have to be a daily occurrence, but your dog will most likely enjoy this time spent together. Most dogs like to go on car journeys and stick their head out of the window. You can make this a special treat for your dog when he has behaved well.

## Play

One of the best ways to develop a bond with your new dog is through play. Taking time out to play games together will encourage him to see you as the leader, which will not only help cement the bonding process but also mark you out as someone he wants to spend time with. Ball

**Bonding rules**
- Regular play.
- Regular exercise.
- Regular feeding times.
- One-on-one time with his owner.
- Be pack leader.
- Never shout or act aggressively.
- Try to have fun together.

games, Frisbee, chase or tug – most dogs love them all. However, always make sure that it is you who calls the shots and ends the session.

## Keep it regular

During any exercise, feeding times, playtime and relaxation, there should not be any issues with the bonding process if these are all part of your daily routine. Whatever you put into your dog in terms of time, love, attention and training, you will get back many times over from the loyalty, companionship and devotion returned to you by your best friend. From the moment you bring him home, they are a good investment.

Spending time together and taking care of your dog will help to form a strong bond.

Bonding With Your New Dog

# CASE STUDY

## CLAUDIA

When Audrey saw an advertisement in her local paper appealing for a home for Claudia, she went straight to the Dogs Trust Kenilworth Centre. The all-black Collie crossbreed had spent five of her seven years in rescue after being taken in as a stray.

'Claudia was muzzled and extremely nervous when I first saw her, but this made me even more determined to adopt her. She looked so sorry for herself but the staff told me that she wasn't a suitable dog for me because I have grandchildren and she always jumped up at people. However, I persevered and got to know her during my 15 visits, which were mostly spent walking round the car park together!

'I'm an experienced owner and have always owned dogs, but it took time to persuade the centre to let me take Claudia home. She was a problem at first as she would not let people into the house, even my family. I taught her to go into the sitting room and watch through the glass door whenever anyone rang the bell. As she slowly came to recognise people, I brought her out on a lead to meet them. I'm still cautious, especially with strangers, but she does accept

| | |
|---:|:---|
| **Age** | 7 years old |
| **Breed** | Crossbreed |
| **Size** | Medium |
| **Colour** | Black |
| **Adopted** | Audrey |

my family now and after barking at them will settle down. Claudia found family life difficult initially – she wasn't used to the sound of the washing machine and vacuum cleaner and wouldn't go out into the garden on her own. When I took her for a walk, she would try to jump under the traffic! She has been with me for 12 months now and although it's been a slow process it's been very rewarding. She nuzzles up to me and follows me wherever I go.

'I already had a rescue dog when I brought Claudia home but poor arthritic Gyp has only got three legs and can't walk far. Luckily, both dogs got on well and Claudia has given Gyp more energy and a real sense of purpose. She hates going out for a walk without him, even though he can't go far. Claudia and I are now inseparable and I can't imagine life without her.'

> **'Claudia is such a sweet-natured dog with so much love to give, but sadly it took seven years for this to be recognised and for her to find a good home.'**

# CHAPTER 4

# TRAINING YOUR DOG

A well-trained dog is a pleasure to own. We all want a dog who behaves appropriately in a crowd, has good manners when we have guests in our home, is reliable around children and never threatening towards other dogs or strangers. The amount of training your dog needs will depend on his background, age, breed and temperament. Whereas some adult rescue dogs will already have some basic training, others will have very little or none at all. If in doubt, always start by teaching the basic commands.

# POSITIVE TRAINING

All dogs can be trained, whether they are puppies or adults, but whereas training a puppy takes lots of time and patience, training an adolescent or adult dog may take much longer and be even harder. This is because puppies are like a dry sponge, ready to soak up anything and everything, whereas an older dog may have had some training or none at all. Adult dogs can be perfect or problematic, carrying the behavioural benefits or baggage of their previous owners.

## Assess your dog

The way in which you approach training your dog will depend on many factors. You will need to take into account his age, breed, ability to listen and learn, and whether he has a dominant or submissive personality. A six-year-old slightly dominant male will need more intensive training than an eight-month-old puppy, because he may have become more 'set' in his ideas. However, all dogs have the capacity to be trained, and therefore the sooner you start the better.

## Make eye contact

One of the most important tricks that you can teach your dog is how to make eye contact with you on command. This can precede anything else you teach him and will act as a signal to him that a training session is about to begin. It also allows him to get to know you better and what you want from him.

Use hand signals as well as treats and verbal commands to train your dog.

You can keep a tasty treat in your hand or pocket to make your dog 'let go'.

**1** With a treat in your hand, call your dog by name – be ready with a verbal signal of your choosing for the command, such as 'Good boy/girl'.

**2** As your dog approaches, let him know that you have a treat by bringing it close enough for him to smell and see it.

**3** Hold the treat up near your eyes (not for too long – maybe 10 seconds) and then reward your dog with the treat.

When your dog does what you want, praise him lavishly and give him treats.

**Note:** If you have a more dominant dog, maintain eye contact with him for only a few seconds. If he shows signs of agitation, stop and try again another day.

## Use rewards

The quickest way to train your dog is to use positive training methods and treats. Remember that you're not asking him to jump through hoops or rescue a drowning person; the commands you are going to teach him will be simple ones, which will make both your lives easier and safer.

- Always use encouragement when training, and only reward your dog with a small treat once he has done – or attempted to perform – the task you have set for him.
- Never use punishment or a raised voice as part of your training regime; this never works and can make matters worse in the long run.

**Training tips**

- Always encourage your dog and never get angry with him.
- Use rewards to reinforce good behaviour and praise him lavishly.
- Don't overdo training. Take it gradually and stick to short 15-minute sessions.
- Never try to train your dog if he is tired or hungry.
- Get the family involved with the commands, so you are all consistent.
- Try to make training enjoyable and fun for both of you.
- If you are getting tired or irritable, stop immediately.

# PLANNING YOUR TRAINING

Like all the other things you do with your dog on a regular basis, sticking to a rigid training routine will ensure success. Try to carry out your sessions at roughly the same time each day, so your dog will expect them, and will be ready and waiting.

## Where?

Training a dog does not have to be restricted to your immediate vicinity. When you are starting out, it's a good idea to have the first few sessions in your house or garden to find out how your dog responds, When he learns what you require of him and you are feeling more confident, try taking him to a local park or some nearby fields to practise your commands. However, be sure to keep your dog on a lead in public places during training.

### Training classes

If you feel that you might struggle with your dog's initial training or he is not responding well, consider joining a local training class. Here you will meet lots of other owners in the same situation as you. Dogs of all ages, shapes and sizes attend training classes every day in the UK, and experts will be on hand to help with any problems you are experiencing. You will also make new friends, and the classes are a great social get-together for new and experienced dog owners.

## When?

There are two specific times during the day that seem to be particularly conducive to successful training for puppies and adult dogs – before and after a meal. Again, you must be consistent and train your dog at the same time each day or every couple of days, starting with short 15-minute training sessions before or after feeding him. Training just before a meal will soon encourage him to believe that if he behaves well he will be given his dinner as a reward; and training about half an hour after a meal can be successful because the dog is content but not tired and full.

## How long?

Keep your puppy training sessions short (10–15 minutes maximum) and consistent, and always make them enjoyable – they should be fun for both of you. The key to shaping your puppy's behaviour is to start out with very easy commands, and to continue to build on these successes with lots of

**1** Teach your dog in easy steps to come to you when called.

**2** When he arrives, teach him to sit or lie down on command.

**3** Always praise him and reward him for his good behaviour when he complies.

repetition. Adult dogs may benefit from slightly longer training sessions of, say, 20–30 minutes. However, never try to force your dog to continue training when he is tired, distracted or bored – it won't work.

## Who should train?

Ideally, start off with one-to-one training sessions with your dog, whether he's a puppy or an adult. It's great to aim for him to take basic commands from all the family eventually, but if everyone tries to teach him, especially if they vary the commands and methods, he will get confused. Train him yourself until he is making progress with the basic commands and then slowly introduce him to accepting familiar ones from other members of the family and even friends.

# 'SIT'

Start off by teaching the 'Sit' command. If your dog can learn to sit on your command, all the other basic training commands will fall into place. As always, make patience and consistency your main objectives, and use some tempting treats to reward correct behaviour. Praise your dog enthusiastically when he does what you want, but if he is having an off day, don't get irritated and shout at him – just stop the session immediately and resume training the following day when he's co-operative.

## What to do…

**1** Call your dog to you and when he is standing in front of you, show him a tasty food treat. Hold it between your finger and thumb, so that he can smell it and even taste it. Get down on his level, if you prefer.

**Training tips**

- Try the 'Sit' command when you and your dog have some quiet time together.
- Always use the command as you raise your hand, so he associates the word with the action of sitting.
- Don't hold the treat too high above your dog's nose or you may encourage him to jump up to get it, which will be counter-productive.
- When he will sit on command, you can move back from him a little and practise it from a short distance away.
- Practise this command in different locations and situations.

**2** Position the treat close to your dog's nose. Slowly lift your hand up and back, so he has to look up to follow your fingers.

**3** Say 'Sit' and as your dog raises his head to look up, his rear end should go down naturally. As soon as his bottom hits the ground and he's in the 'sit' position, give him the treat and then praise him really enthusiastically.

**Note:** If he fails to do this or is not sitting correctly, don't give the treat. Try again until he gets it right.

# 'COME'

Coming to you when he is called is one of the most important skills your dog can learn. This command can help to prevent and defuse any number of potentially difficult and dangerous situations. On a more practical level, the command will give him more opportunities for free running because you can be confident that he will return to you when you call him in any environment. Keep the training sessions short and always offer rewards for positive reinforcement of this behaviour. Ideally, he shouldn't be given any freedom in public places until he has proved his dependability at coming when called.

## Training tips

- Start in the house, training your dog in different rooms before practising outside in the garden.
- Try to make your voice sound exciting; if your dog does not respond, get down to his level and clap your hands or pat your knees.
- Make it fun: use a whistle or a favourite toy to encourage him.
- Call him to you at unusual moments in the house, and then in the garden, to help reinforce the command.
- When you have established a consistently positive reaction to your command, take your dog to a quiet park or field to test him.
- Use a helper and ask them to hold your dog while you move slowly away from them. From a distance, show him the treat in your hand and then call him to you as your friend releases him.
- Never reprimand him – your dog is coming to you because he wants a reward for his good behaviour, so don't shout or he will think he is being told off for coming to you.
- When he comes on command, ask him to 'Sit' before giving him a treat.

## What to do...

**1** Ask your dog to 'Sit' and you stand only a couple of steps away from him. Show him a tasty treat and move your hand around excitedly to get him interested in it.

**2** Call him to you by saying 'Come' or his name. As soon as he comes to you, give him the treat and praise him lavishly.

**3** Gradually increase the distance between you, praising and rewarding him every time he comes to you when called.

**When all else fails...**
If your dog will not come when he is called, you can attach a training line to his collar and gently haul him in. As soon as he gets to you, praise and treat him. He will soon learn that coming when called will lead to rewards.

# 'STAY'

You are now well on your way to having a well-trained dog. Once 'Sit' and 'Come' are under your belt, it's time to turn him into an even better behaved companion by teaching him the 'Stay' command. Although this may prove more difficult than teaching him to sit or come, it is not an overly complicated process, and patience and regular practice will pay dividends. The 'Stay' is very useful in all sorts of situations, including opening the front door or taking hot dishes out of the oven.

## Training tips

- If you wish, you can reinforce this command by using a hand signal. Hold your hand up, with the flat of the hand towards your dog, when you give the command. Keep your hand raised in this way with his gaze focused on it while you move slowly away from him.
- Gradually increase the distance between you and your dog. Always remain in his sight until he understands how to stay. Eventually you can even try leaving the room after giving the command.
- Practise starting this command in the standing position. If successful, your dog should not change positions during the 'Stay' command.
- Once he has mastered the 'Stay', you can try practising it with various distractions. Get a friend to talk or squeeze a squeaky toy. Your dog should not move at all despite the distractions.
- When outside without a lead, make sure you are in a fenced-in area.
- When your dog becomes an expert at staying on command, you will no longer need to give him a treat every time – only occasionally. However, rewarding with praise is always a good idea.

### Caution!
Never leave your dog sitting in the 'Stay' position for long periods or go away and forget about him, especially when he is in a public space, such as a park or field. You may inadvertently put him in danger if he suddenly decides to bolt or if he is attacked by another dog or 'rescued' by a well-meaning stranger.

## What to do…

**1** Start by attaching a lead to your dog's collar. Tell him to 'Sit'. When he is sitting, praise him and give him a treat, but keep him sitting.

**2** Say your dog's name, followed by 'Stay'. After a couple of seconds, praise and treat him for staying in a sit.

**3** Release him from the command by saying 'OK' and encouraging him to move. Repeat this daily, with the length of stay increasing to 15 seconds or more. Then try slowly moving away from your dog. Facing him, repeat the 'Stay' command as you back away. Praise him if you can move a few feet away from him while he sits still.

# 'DOWN'

The 'Down' command is as simple as teaching your dog to sit. It is extremely useful for calming him down when he becomes over-excited or is in a hectic or distracting environment, as well as for keeping him in the 'Stay' for longer periods of time.

## What to do...

**1** With your dog sitting in front of you or beside you, get his attention by showing him a treat in your hand.

**2** Holding the treat in front of his nose say his name followed by the word 'Down'. As you do this, slowly move the treat down between his legs towards the ground.

**3** He should move his front legs forward until his elbows touch the ground and he is lying down in the correct position. When this happens, praise and reward him immediately.

**Jumping up**
Don't ever use the command 'Down' to stop your dog jumping up – this will confuse him as he will associate the word with the action of lying down.

# 'FETCH'

Teaching your dog to fetch a ball, toy or any object is good fun. Once he has learnt how to do this, he will spend hours retrieving items in order to please you… and to make you throw them again. Your dog will learn to bring you anything you throw for him, as long as he can get it in his mouth!

## What to do…

**1** Tease your dog with a toy he likes to attract his attention.

**2** As soon as you have his full and undivided attention, ask him to 'Fetch' and throw the toy a short distance away.

**3** Your dog should run to the toy and pick it up. Encourage him to run back to you with the toy in his mouth. Gently retrieve it – don't grab it but get him to drop it at your feet or give it to you. Praise and treat him, then throw it again.

**Carry a ball**
Let your dog carry a ball, a soft object or a toy in his mouth on your daily walks in order to get him used to carrying something. He will enjoy doing this.

# 'HEEL'

There's nothing worse than being dragged along by your dog on the end of a lead. We've all laughed at people who look like they are being 'walked by their dog' instead of the other way round, but there are easy ways to train your dog to walk calmly by your side. This transforms walking him into an easy and enjoyable pastime, and you'll look forward to your time together in the great outdoors. Your objective in this training exercise is to have him walk beside you on a loose lead.

## What to do…

**1** With your dog on a lead, ask him to sit by your side. Have some tasty treats concealed in your other hand.

**2** Walk slowly forwards and say 'Heel'. If he walks with you (without pulling forward or hanging back) reward him with praise and a treat.

**3** If he races ahead or hangs back, put him back into the sitting position beside you and start again.

**Note:** Each time you practise this, try to go a little further with your dog walking nicely by your side. Always praise and treat him for good behaviour.

## Training tips

- If your dog tries to race ahead, step in front of him and then make him stop and sit before trying again. You should always be in control.
- As you walk, try patting the top of your leg or your hip to indicate where you want him to be
- Keep his attention focused exclusively on you, using the treats to encourage him to stay close to your side.
- Say the word 'Heel' as often as possible while he is performing the task correctly. He will learn to associate the action with the command.
- Never drag your dog forward or pull sharply back on his lead.
- Be patient and he will eventually understand what you want.

**Collars**

Never use a chain collar or choke chain to walk your dog. These collars are cruel and can damage his throat and larynx if he keeps pulling or you jerk on the lead. Use an appropriate leather, nylon or fabric collar. For it to fit comfortably, you should be able to insert two fingers easily.

# CASE STUDY

## BENJI

When Jan saw Benji's photograph and details on the Dogs Trust stand at her local County Show she thought he looked really sweet. 'We love Terriers but as we already had four dogs we had no plans to adopt another. However, when we went to Dogs Trust Bridgend open day, we saw that Benji was still there and he looked so depressed, unresponsive and sad. We decided that if there was any way in which we could help him we would try to do so. We hoped that we could offer him the ideal home where he could be happy.

'I think Benji is a cross between a Fox Terrier and a Jack Russell, and, although I love all dogs, Jack Russell types are so special. It took him a few weeks to adjust to living with us and the other dogs. At first he was a loner and didn't join in much: he would growl and snarl if you came too close and he felt afraid. He even bit us on a few occasions when we didn't give him the space he needed and we didn't read the signs.

'We needed to help Benji to learn to trust us – he had been in the kennels for over two years, so it took some time. However, day by day, he is

| | |
|---:|:---|
| **Age** | 8 years old |
| **Breed** | Terrier cross |
| **Size** | Small |
| **Colour** | Tricolour |
| **Adopted** | Jan |

now making good and steady progress and gradually seems to be much more relaxed and is giving us a little bit more of himself.

'Living in the countryside on a farm has definitely helped him because he can stay busy all day long. He loves hunting for rats and mice in the barns and stables. At first he did this from dawn till dusk and we let him do his own thing. Now he joins us at lunchtime and comes for a walk with the other dogs. He loves being outside but he wants someone to be with him. To help him settle in, we gave him his own beds in different places where he could be away from the other dogs. We let him decide what he wanted to do. We also talked to him a lot; he is an amazingly intelligent little man and he does listen to you. He picks things up very quickly.'

'It is such a privilege to share your life with any of these beautiful rescue dogs. They fill your life with so much love and laughter as well as lots of dirt!'

# CHAPTER 5

# GOOD DOG BEHAVIOUR

No new owner would expect every rescue dog or puppy to come home with them without some initial problems. Whilst all rescue centres will never allow an overly-dominant or aggressive dog to be rehomed with a family, some dogs may still have behaviour problems. Don't assume that you cannot cope with a less than perfect dog – you can. And remember that you are now responsible for his wellbeing and happiness, and the satisfaction of seeing the end result will be better than you ever imagined.

# WHAT TO EXPECT

Rescue dogs can be desperately in need of affection and attention. There are many who have been abused, neglected, malnourished or abandoned. In these cases, the dogs can appear skittish and distrustful of humans as well as other animals. Some people think that they will always be wary of humans, and this belief tends to limit their likelihood of being adopted. However, most rescue dogs can make loving and grateful companions after you have gained their trust. The following suggestions will better prepare you for caring for your new friend, and, with patience, you will see positive improvements in your dog within the first few weeks.

## At first

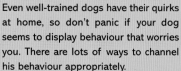

Your new four-legged friend may not be very playful and loving at first – everything will be new and strange to him and it takes time to settle in to unfamiliar surroundings with new people. Indeed, he may not have had the opportunity to play or to love his previous owner without punishment. If this is the case, you must expect him to be nervous and mistrustful

**Don't worry!**
Most dogs need us to guide their behaviour.
Even well-trained dogs have their quirks at home, so don't panic if your dog seems to display behaviour that worries you. There are lots of ways to channel his behaviour appropriately.

initially. Give him time and let him learn for himself that you are not going to hurt him; you can't rush him into being your new friend. Always try to appear non-threatening, be patient and never use any force.

## Gentle approach

Rescue dogs that have been abused will often cower down when they are approached. If your dog does this, be patient and adopt a gentle approach. Instead of coming towards him face on, try approaching him by walking backwards with your palm up and hand outstretched behind you to make him feel less threatened. As he begins to realise that you mean him no harm, you will be able to start approaching him face on.

## Why?

As we saw earlier on, dogs can be in rescue for various reasons: the death of their owners, marriage break-ups, families who have lost interest in their new puppy, allergies, abandonment and, in some cases, cruelty. Whatever the reason, bear in mind that they may be confused and will no doubt be wondering what is happening to them. They may well find it hard to put their trust into someone else, and this is a perfectly natural state of mind.

Introduce your new dog to other dogs in a controlled and calm situation.

## Not all the same

Of course, lots of dogs sail through life with an easy-going personality and a seemingly endless ability to enjoy themselves and to take everything in their stride. They will quickly settle into their new home, trusting and loving everyone they meet and displaying very few (or no) signs of their past at all.

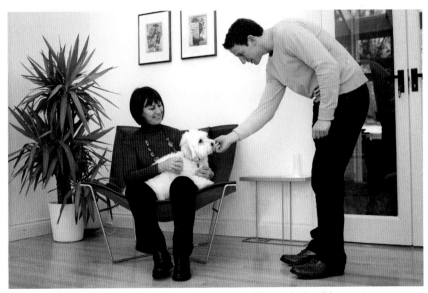

Make your dog feel safe and hold him reassuringly if introducing him to strangers.

# COMMON PROBLEMS

Most experienced owners should be familiar with behaviour problems, but they can be worrying if you've never owned a dog before. Barking, biting, chewing and other common behaviours are often mishandled by novice owners, but understanding how and why they occur is the first step to solving and preventing them.

## Barking

Dogs bark to tell us something. Excessive barking can be a nuisance, so work out why your dog is barking to avoid the situations where it occurs.

- Never shout at your dog to stop him barking – it won't work.
- Try to eliminate the cause; for example, let your dog into or out of the house, answer the door, or take the toy off him.
- If there seems to be no reason for the barking, clap your hands and say 'Quiet'. If he stops barking, praise him and play a game to distract him.
- Never make a big fuss of your dog if he is barking; he will take this as affirmation that he is doing the right thing.

## Chewing

This is a natural behaviour for dogs, but if it becomes a problem the time has come to teach your dog to do something more acceptable instead.

- Encourage him to chew on acceptable edible chews and toys.
- Put your personal possessions away safely; when you're not at home, confine your dog to an area where less destruction can be caused.
- If you catch him in the act of chewing the wrong thing, quickly correct him with a sharp noise and then replace the item with a chew toy.
- Exercise relieves boredom, which is one of the main causes of chewing.

## Begging

It's easy to encourage this behaviour, albeit innocently, by tossing leftovers to your dog. Dogs beg because they love food, but table scraps are not treats. It's hard to resist that longing look, but giving in will create future problems.

- Before you sit down to eat, tell your dog to stay, preferably where he cannot stare at you – if necessary, confine him to another room.

Discourage 'play biting' by offering an exciting toy or a tasty treat if he tries to bite.

- If he tries to beg, just ignore him.
- If he behaves, give him a special treat after you have finished eating.

## Biting

Puppies love biting things, including hands, when they are teething, but they can be trained to regulate this behaviour. Adult dogs should not bite; if yours 'play bites', stop it immediately. Catch this problem early and it's easy to rectify.

- With a young puppy, redirect the biting to a toy or chew bone. As soon as he bites your hands, say 'No!' and replace your fingers with the chew.
- Make him think he is hurting you. Startle him with your voice, then pull away and stop playing. He will learn that when he bites, the fun ends.
- You can teach an older puppy or adult dog the command 'Leave it!'.
- If your dog has a serious biting problem or appears aggressive rather than playful, contact the rescue centre for advice.

# ANXIETY

It's easy to fall into the trap of giving your new rescue dog 150 per cent of your time and love when he arrives, thereby creating the wrong impression of your daily routine. Many new owners take a week's holiday to help their dog settle in, taking him for walks and playing games, but when they return to work he gets stressed and anxious when he's left on his own.

## Separation anxiety

If you leave the house does your dog cry constantly until you return? And when you come back, has your home been trashed? If so, he may be suffering from separation anxiety, a very common problem, which is easy to address. Many

dogs end up back in rescue due to this, but this problem can be resolved successfully. Dogs love their owners and they will quickly develop a close relationship with them. However, this closeness can leave them confused and frightened when they are left in the house on their own.

- Prepare your dog for your departure. Don't lavish attention on him before leaving. However well intended, this only makes your departure more noticeable.
- Instead of petting and kissing him goodbye, prepare him for your absence by reducing interaction immediately before you depart.

A toy can distract your dog when you're leaving.

- Try ignoring your dog for several minutes to make your departure less stressful and decrease his anxiety. Don't say 'Goodbye' to him.
- Just before you go out of the door, provide distractions, such as a new toy, or leave a radio or television turned on for background noise.

## The shy or fearful dog

Shyness and/or timidity may develop as a young dog matures. It may be caused by poor socialisation during puppyhood, emotional trauma, physical abuse or not getting enough social interaction. Shyness and fear can lead to aggression and biting, but there are lots of ways to solve this behaviour and transform your dog into a happy and confident companion.

### What are the signs?

Tell-tale signs include defensive behaviour, such as guarding toys or shrinking back when being approached; aggression around other dogs and/or people; discomfort in public places; constant barking and/or growling; uncontrollable panting; and a desire to be left alone, particularly in busy social situations.

### How you can help

- When meeting new people, always hold your dog close to make him feel secure. Make sure that the stranger approaches slowly with their hand outstretched, avoiding direct eye contact, and strokes the dog under the chin, not on top of his head.
- Introduce your dog to others on a one-to-one basis, starting with one small dog. Don't take him to the park until he gets used to new dogs.
- Expose him to a variety of environments and if something makes him fearful or anxious, just ignore it. Making a big deal of it will only make it worse. If you fuss, your dog may think he's supposed to react that way.
- Massage can calm and relax your dog's nervous system, minimising his anxiety.
- Lastly, never try to force him into situations that are not comfortable for him. Walk away and try again another day.

**Reducing anxiety**
Even well-trained dogs can be transformed into destructive troublemakers as a result of separation anxiety. Training away this difficulty can be hard, especially when a dog feels very connected to his owner, but by preparing him and using appropriate, immediate and lasting distractions, you can reduce his anxiety until it's not a problem.

# AGGRESSION

There are many different types of aggression, and your dog may display aggressive behaviour for lots of different reasons, including defensive or fear-induced aggression, a reaction to punishment, pain or dominance, or possessive, territorial or sexual (male-to-male or female-to-female) aggression.

## Recognising the signs

An aggressive dog will stand up on his toes and may have raised hackles (the fur on and around the back of his neck); he may carry his tail high and wag it slowly; and he may growl. Any of these traits may be displayed to humans or other dogs. If this happens, you must deal with his behaviour immediately.

### Dog-to-dog aggression

This usually occurs when you are out walking your dog on a collar and lead. To teach him that it's not acceptable, ask a friend to bring a dog to your house – the dog must be friendly.

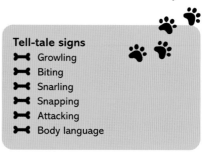

**Tell-tale signs**
- Growling
- Biting
- Snarling
- Snapping
- Attacking
- Body language

**1** Ask your friend to put their dog on a lead and stand with him.
**2** Put your dog on his lead, and walk past the other dog. Stay relaxed; if you feel stress, your dog will be stressed.
**3** Leave about 6m (20ft) between the two dogs as you pass by. Continue walking and don't stop – you are in control of this situation, not your dog.
**4** The moment your dog begins to react to the other dog, issue a correction. This could be a tug on the lead, a sideways bump, or anything that permits you to continue walking without stopping and breaks his concentration.
**5** Repeat until he walks past the other dog without a reaction, and continue practising this on a regular basis until you feel that he has been desensitised.

### Dog-to-human aggression

It is very unlikely that a rescue dog that displayed any form of aggression would end up in a family home. Rescue organisations have stringent tests to ensure that only dogs with steady and reliable temperaments are offered for

To curb dog-to-dog aggression, practise walking your dog on a lead past a friend's dog.

rehoming. Fear is the most likely reason for a rescue dog to show aggression towards a human, often because he has been treated badly in a former home. He may be wary of certain people, such as bearded men or children, because he associates being hurt with someone he physically recognises. If your dog displays signs of aggressive behaviour to humans, rule out any medical reasons with your vet and contact the rescue centre for advice.

## How to combat aggression

- Identify the situations in which your dog shows aggressive behaviour. If they are not obvious, you may need the help of a canine behaviourist, as the cause of aggression isn't always evident to the untrained eye.
- Avoid doing anything that could trigger aggression. Seemingly harmless actions, such as hugging your dog, could be a trigger. If the fur on his back rises, his ears lie flat, his eyes focus sharply, or his teeth are showing, his dog language is telling you to disengage from the situation.
- Hand out praise and treats when he displays friendly behaviour.
- Never cuddle him for showing aggression, even to comfort him.
- Never punish him as this will lead to increased aggressive behaviour. Positive reinforcement gets the best results and develops the pet-owner bond, thereby diminishing and preventing aggressive behaviour.
- Feeding your dog a teaspoon of honey a day with his meal may be an old wives' tale, but some people swear that it works.
- If you are worried, contact your rescue centre or vet straight away.

# MINOR PROBLEMS

There are lots of minor but annoying behaviour problems that owners sometimes experience with their new pooch. Luckily, these are all preventable – all you need is patience and to act positively and consistently to prevent the bad behaviour.

## Housetraining worries

Most adult rescue dogs are housetrained and will let you know when they need the toilet by standing at the door or barking. However, there are some dogs who may need a little help, especially puppies, ex-racing Greyhounds who have lived in kennels all their lives, long-stay residents from a shelter, who may have become used to a kennel routine, rescue dogs who were picked up as strays, and dogs who have suffered stress and may have 'forgotten' what to do.

### Potty training

It makes no difference whether you are training a puppy or an adult dog; the method for toilet training is exactly the same for all ages.

- Select a toilet area in your garden and always use the same 'patch'.
- Let your dog have a sniff and – if he does his business there – praise and reward him to encourage him to repeat the behaviour.
- Make sure you put him out first thing in the morning, after food, on waking, when he sniffs the floor, after play and before going to bed.
- Take a puppy outside once every two hours.
- Take an adult dog out once an hour.
- Never reprimand him for the odd accident inside. If you catch him in the act, take him out at once.
- Be consistent or your dog will get confused.

Always clean up after your dog, especially in any public spaces.

# Digging

Dogs have an instinct to dig, especially some Terriers. Digging can be their idea of fun; they may want to bury (or dig up) something or they may simply be bored. If you have a garden that you'd rather not have turned into an excavation site by a dog that loves to dig, try one or more of the following.

- Dogs often dig because they are bored. Entertain your dog with toys and playing games and make sure he gets lots of vigorous exercise.
- If your dog loves to dig, why not create an area in your garden where it is acceptable for him to do so? Fence off the designated area and fill it with earth or even sand. Bury treats to encourage your dog to use it.
- You can discourage him from digging by burying a layer of chicken wire (available from hardware shops) just under the surface of the soil. The dog won't like the feel of the wire on his feet.
- Try putting cayenne pepper or hot chilli sauce in his holes.
- Remove temptation: dogs enjoy digging in fresh earth, so if you are working in your garden, remove fresh soil from your dog's reach with a fence or covering.
- Dig it yourself! Go out and dig up any bones or other things your dog has buried, but don't let him see you do this. Fill the holes back in.

Many dogs love digging, so give yours an area where it's acceptable to dig.

# DOGS AND CARS

Lots of dogs like nothing more than a ride out in the car and regard a trip to the park or beach as a real treat. However, a rescue dog may never have travelled in a car before, and it is your job to make sure it's fun and stress-free for both of you.

## Try it out

If you are uncertain about how your dog will react to being in a car, start by sitting in a stationary car with him. Encourage him to sit in the back while you stay in front. Try starting up the engine and putting the radio on, and watch his reaction carefully. Only praise very calm and normal behaviour; if he gets distressed, don't use praise but remove him from the car straight away. If you keep repeating this exercise, your nervous dog will start feeling happy about being in the car with you.

### Travel safely
- Don't offer food treats: they may make your dog sick.
- Keep his collar and identification tag on whenever you are driving.
- A dog can get heat stroke in a parked car very quickly. Never ever leave your dog unattended in warm weather for any length of time.
- Pack water, toys and a blanket for him when you go on a long journey.
- Consult your vet if he shows any signs of car sickness.
- If you don't have an estate car, you can purchase a special dog safety harness or use a crate.

Most dogs love getting in the car if it leads to a walk.

## Go for a ride

As soon as your dog feels confident about getting in the car, take him for a short journey. You could drive to some nearby countryside or a local park. Try to make the end result enjoyable as you want your dog to make the association of being in the car with having a good time.

# DOGS AND CHASING

It's great fun to teach your dog to chase a ball, but if he chases inappropriate things he can become a nuisance. Herding breeds sometimes chase livestock while sight hounds may chase potential prey, such as smaller dogs and cats; some dogs even chase cyclists and cars, which could lead to an accident.

## What you can do

If your dog is a chaser, you need to anticipate trouble, which means spotting situations before he does, and calling him to you if he is off the lead before he goes into a mad dash. You will also need to channel his chasing instincts into a more appropriate outlet and teach him to chase toys instead.

Greyhounds are sight hounds who love to chase, so focus their attention on you.

-  Always keep your dog on the lead if temptation is likely.
- Expose him to as many triggers as possible when he is on the lead, and reward him for staying still and paying attention to you.
- Make him sit beside you for a few minutes by a busy road – practise this regularly until he gets used to the traffic passing by.
- If you have a cat, or a friend who owns one, ask your dog to sit quietly with you while the cat is nearby. Be sure to praise him all the time that his attention is focused on you and not the cat.
- Spend some time each day playing chasing fun games with your dog, throwing toys or balls for him to chase and bring back to you on your command. This enables him to use his natural instincts appropriately.

# CASE STUDY

## FLO AND ELFIE

**Helen and Peter had always had rescue dogs, and when their dog Stan died, their other dog Max pined and the vet advised them to get him a companion. She said that the Dogs Trust always try to find the right dog for each owner – and that proved to be the case.**

'As Max is not very dominant and getting on in years, we wanted a bitch, and on the website we found Flo, who had been abandoned. She almost smiled in her photograph and her profile was perfect. When we went to meet her, it was love at first sight! Here was this solid little dog for whom the phrase "bundle of joy" could have been invented. She was, and still is, *thrilled* with life. She is so enthusiastic and adores us. But, despite her ebullience, she is insecure: she runs for miles but never lets you out of her sight. She is such a softie and wants to touch all the time.

'At the Dogs Trust, we saw a pathetic, emaciated Jack Russell/Collie cross. She had obviously had a very hard life, suffered from a food allergy that had never been treated and had lost all the fur on the lower half of her body. One ear was damaged, her skin was crusted and sore, her back legs and tail wonky, and every vertebra

| Name | Flo |
|---|---|
| Age | 4 years old |
| Breed | Staffordshire Bull Terrier |
| Size | Medium |
| Colour | White |

| Name | Elfie |
|---|---|
| Age | 10 years old |
| Breed | Cross breed |
| Size | Small |
| Colour | Black and white |

visible. She was in a desperate state and we had to take her home. It was a magical moment when she met Flo and Max and played happily with them. She never looked back and they became friends. Routine is key and we make sure everyone is treated the same and each dog respects the others' space.

'Elfie is now a totally different dog. When she came to us she couldn't bear to be petted as her skin was so sore but our vet designed a treatment programme and special diet and she has put on weight and her skin is clear. She is a confident dog who enjoys life to the full. Don't worry about having more than one dog, or one with special needs. Watching our dogs running outside or curled up by the fire is heart warming and they are no more bother than one dog.'

'Before taking a dog home, adopters attend a training session. We thought this was excellent and helpful, even for experienced dog owners like us.'

# CHAPTER 6

# KEEPING YOUR DOG HAPPY

A happy dog is the perfect companion for you and your family. As well as the obvious daily requirements – a healthy diet, lots of exercise and a solid routine – he will thrive on mental stimulation, good health care and lots of love. Many behavioural problems stem from boredom, so spending time with your dog is important, whether you're out walking, playing games, grooming him or just relaxing together at home on the sofa.

# HOW TO HAVE A CONTENTED DOG

Early training is important. No matter how old your rescue dog is, you must start working with him from the day he steps through your door. Believe it or not, a dog who understands the basic commands and his place in the home will rarely give you any trouble.

## Exercise

Plenty of physical exercise will leave your dog feeling happy and content. He will eat better, sleep soundly and behave better when he has a good exercise routine. Aim to give him at least one good walk a day (more for larger or more energetic dogs) and, if he will come back to you, some free-running, too.

All dogs love to play and free-running exercise will make them fitter and stronger.

## Bonding

The bond that is formed between a human and a dog is one of the strongest known to man. The best way to do this is to show your dog love and respect, provide him with clear boundaries, and spend time stroking and handling him. Don't worry if you feel that you haven't immediately bonded with him – it takes time to get to know each other.

## Diet

Try to establish set feeding times for your dog as soon as he arrives. Give him familiar food that you know he is used to eating – the rehoming centre will advise you on a healthy diet and which brands he likes. Use treats as just that – treats. Too many given randomly will cause weight gain if you are not careful.

Rain or shine, whatever the weather, you must take your dog out for a daily walk or some free-running.

**Working families**
There is no reason why you cannot work and still have a happy dog. Make sure you leave him fresh water and lots of toys while you are out. If you are out all day, however, ask a friend or neighbour (or even a professional dog walker) to pop in and take him for a walk or play a game in the garden and provide him with some company.

# A HEALTHY DIET

Dogs are happy to eat the same food at the same time every day for their entire lives – they don't need variety. At first, give your dog whatever he was fed at the rescue centre to avoid potential tummy upsets, especially while he is coping with adjusting to his new environment and may be feeling stressed.

## Which food?

There are three types of food that you can offer, and each one has its own benefits. It's important to choose the one that suits you and your dog.

- **Complete dry food:** this comes in the form of dried pellets and needs no preparation. Most dried foods contain all the nutrients that your dog needs, and some have added essential oils, rice and vegetables.
- **Canned food:** a moist meat-based food in a can. This can be fed on its own or with a mixer. Again, it is very convenient and easy to feed.
- **Fresh food:** this includes mincemeat, tripe, offal, chicken or any meat. It can be mixed with vegetables, rice, pasta or a mixer. This is a favourite of many owners, but it does take more time to prepare and cook.

**Signs of a good diet**

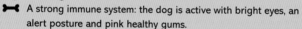

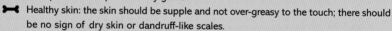

- A strong immune system: the dog is active with bright eyes, an alert posture and pink healthy gums.
- Healthy skin: the skin should be supple and not over-greasy to the touch; there should be no sign of dry skin or dandruff-like scales.
- Glossy coat: in longer-coated breeds, the coat should have a lovely sheen and be free from odour; in harsh-coated breeds, it should feel nice to touch.
- Good body condition: the dog's ribs should be well covered and he shouldn't appear overweight or underweight – if you are not sure, check with your vet.
- Good digestion: your dog's faeces should be firm and not too smelly; if he has sloppy motions or very smelly ones, alter his diet slowly to see if the condition improves.

# Changing your dog's food

If you wish to change what you are feeding your dog, take things slowly. Start by adding a little of the new food to his usual meal, and then gradually reduce the old food as you add more of the new. Over a week or so, you should be able to change his food completely.

Ask your dog to wait patiently while you prepare his food and put it down for him.

# THE IMPORTANCE OF EXERCISE

While every breed requires a different amount of exercise, the universal rule that is true for all dogs, no matter what shape, size, age or breed, is that some daily activity and exercise are essential for keeping their physical and emotional health at an optimum level. Lack of exercise can lead to obesity, heart problems and bone and joint disorders, as well as behaviour problems, including barking, stress, anxiety and boredom.

## What sort of exercise?

There are many ways to exercise your dog, and it can be beneficial to vary them and not to stick to the same old ones all the time. Walking on the lead, jogging, playing games together, roadwork and free-running are all great ways to keep him healthy. Choose the ones that you both enjoy and fit easiest into your lifestyle and environment – that way, you are more likely to build some exercise into your daily routine and even to look forward to it.

Give your dog the freedom to enjoy running and playing in a safe environment.

# How much?

The amount of exercise a dog needs will vary enormously, depending on his size, breed, health and age. Larger dogs generally need a lot more than

You will both enjoy your daily walks together and will reap the mutual health benefits.

smaller ones – at least 40 minutes a day. However, some big dogs such as Greyhounds and Irish Wolfhounds need surprisingly little, whereas smaller, energetic Jack Russells and other Terriers are almost impossible to tire out. Many Spaniels and Collies can walk and run for miles and, like most herding and working dogs and gundogs, also need more active and focused movement. They will enjoy playing games of fetch with a ball and Frisbee. Many smaller breeds, such as companion Toy dogs, should be given two to three short walks per day. As you get to know your dog, you will discover what works best for him and fits into your daily routine.

## Why exercise?

- An active dog rarely has digestive problems, especially if he has a healthy, well-balanced diet.
- A dog who is walked daily will be less susceptible to infections.
- An active dog is less likely to get depressed and will probably live longer.
- Exercise reduces stress and will make your dog sleep well. Dogs, like humans, can suffer from insomnia, and exercise is usually prescribed as the most effective cure.
- Regular and sufficient exercise prevents obesity in you and your dog.
- It can help to prevent unwanted behaviour by distracting your dog and tiring him out.
- It builds confidence by putting your dog in different social situations.

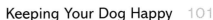

# PLAYING WITH YOUR DOG

As well as regular exercise, you also need to spend time with your dog just playing together and stimulating him mentally. Like people, dogs get bored when they have nothing to do. They enjoy social interaction, being given specific tasks and learning new games and how to perform tricks.

## Which toys?

It's important to choose toys of a suitable type, size and weight for your dog. Whereas some dogs love chasing and fetching, others prefer tug games or playing with squeaky toys. When you go into your local pet store, there will be an amazing range of toys on offer, so here are some guidelines to help you choose the right ones for your dog.

- Toys with small parts are sometimes dangerous; if your dog prefers playing with a squeaky toy, check that it's safe and can't be dismantled.
- Never buy a toy that is smaller than the back of your dog's throat.
- Watch your dog: does he prefer chasing games or chewing games?
- Soft toys are either treated like a baby by your dog, or ripped to shreds within minutes. Try one out and see what happens.
- Treat him to a dental health toy – this will clean his teeth while he plays.
- Interactive toys are good fun. Frisbees and tug-ropes will enable you to join in and enjoy the game, too.

## What to play inside

There are lots of games that you can play inside the house with your dog. Make sure you have a variety of toys and use them as part of your playtime. Hide and seek is always popular and very easy – all you have to do is to hide one of your dog's favourite toys and then encourage him to find it.

Alternatively, you can try placing three plastic cups upside-down on the floor or a low table and hiding a treat under one of them for your dog to sniff out and find. Repeat several times, placing the treat under different cups. Some dogs, especially the bull breeds, love tug-of-war games where each of you has an end to the rope. However, never play these games with a dog who is undergoing training with you for aggressive behavioural problems. And make sure that it is always you who wins the last game.

## What to play outside

Playing games outside in the garden or park is a good way to exercise your dog at the same time as having some fun. Here are some great ideas for you to try out together.

**Remember...**
- Always stop the game as soon as your dog becomes bored.
- Always reward good behaviour.
- Never let a confident dog 'win' all the time; allow a nervous or under-confident dog to win sometimes.

- **Frisbee:** get one or two Frisbees and spend time throwing them and watching your dog chase them through the air.
- **Fetch:** use your voice commands to play chase the ball or a favourite toy and ask your dog to 'Fetch' it back to you.
- **Treasure hunt:** try hiding a few tasty treats around the garden and ask your dog to search for them. Most dogs love playing this game.
- **Hula hoop:** place a hula-hoop on the ground and, using a treat as a reward, teach your dog to stand in the circle and 'Stay'.

Terriers have amazing energy and vitality, and they love playing games with toys.

# FUN ACTIVITIES TO ENJOY WITH YOUR DOG

There are so many activities in which you and your dog can participate. You can have great fun together if you join one of the specialist canine clubs and enter competitions and shows.

## Companion Dog Shows (CDS)

These shows are held under the rules of the Kennel Club (the UK's governing body of all things canine) and are often organised by dog clubs or charities to raise money for good causes. Classes such as the Most Handsome Dog, Prettiest Bitch and Best Rescue are usually on offer. Check on the internet to see if a show is being held soon near you and go along with your dog.

## Agility

One of the most popular canine activities in the world, this discipline involves getting your dog to jump over hurdles, run through hoops and overcome all manner of obstacles against the clock. Many rescue dogs are very good at agility, and, indeed, some go on to win competitions at a high level. Look on the internet or in the phonebook for local clubs. Many dogs love doing agility and it's a good way for you to keep fit, too, and meet new friends.

Dogs just love the excitement of agility.

## Dancing with dogs

This really fun activity gives you the opportunity to strut your stuff alongside your canine partner. The basics of dancing with your dog (often called Heelwork to Music) involve training him to move alongside you and perform certain moves with you... all to a piece of music. Dogs have successfully danced to songs ranging from *The*

Agility gives owners and dogs the opportunity to have fun and bond together.

*Sorcerer's Apprentice* to *Dancing Queen*. If your dog has learnt some basic commands already, you can try this out at home before looking for local classes. It's a particularly great activity for small, agile dogs and Collie types.

## Flyball

This game is very similar to agility and requires a dog to chase a ball over an assault course in the fastest time possible. Its name is derived from the fact that sometimes the dogs literally fly in the air after the ball! This is another activity where crossbreeds shine. Although it requires considerable training and commitment, it's great fun and gives you the chance to meet other dog owners. There are lots of clubs, so go along and have a look.

## Good Citizens Dog Scheme

The Kennel Club Good Citizen Dog Scheme is the largest dog training scheme in the UK. Its aim is to promote responsible dog ownership and, in turn, to enhance your relationship with your dog and also make the wider community aware of the benefits associated with owning one. Classes are run all over the country and usually last for about 12 weeks. You can receive Gold, Silver and Bronze awards if you participate in the scheme. For more details, go on the Kennel Club's website and find out what is on offer in your area.

# HOLIDAY TIME

We all like to take a break, and many hotels, guesthouses and cottages will happily allow dogs to join you on your holiday. You need to plan your vacations (with or without your dog) well in advance, so that all the necessary arrangements can be made and you can have a relaxing, stress-free break together.

## Taking your dog with you

If you do not like the thought of leaving your dog in the care of others, consider taking him with you. However, do check the following:

- Contact the hotel to ensure that they are happy to accept dogs.
- Ask if your dog will be allowed in your bedroom.
- Ask which areas of the hotel your dog will have access to.
- Find out if there is an area nearby for walking your dog.
- Check that there are no extra or hidden charges for dogs.
- Pack extra bedding for your dog plus food if not provided by the hotel.

**Out of bounds**
Many seaside resorts do not allow dogs on beaches during the period from late spring to early autumn, while others restrict you to the extremities of the beach. There are also restrictions in many inland holiday destinations and National Parks in the UK, so make sure that you do your research carefully before booking your holiday.

## Leaving your dog behind

Some holidays are not suitable for dogs, especially if you're planning to travel overseas, although the introduction of Pet Passports has made this possible. Don't feel guilty about leaving your dog behind – thousands of people do this every year, and it doesn't make you a bad owner. Dogs are usually happiest being looked after in their own home by a family member or friend, but if this is not possible, you may have to consider boarding kennels as an option.

### Boarding kennels

Many boarding kennels nowadays are like a home from home, and the staff are specially trained in how to care for, exercise and feed your dog to your requirements. Ask dog-owning friends if they can recommend some local kennels, as word of mouth is usually a good guide. Search the internet to find some kennels you like the look of, then telephone and ask if you can arrange to go and see them. Always visit before booking your dog in – this gives you the opportunity to look at their facilities, meet the staff and form your own opinions. Remember that your dog will have to be up-to-date with all his vaccinations and you will probably be asked to provide certification of this.

Your dog may enjoy going to the seaside and walking on the beach with you.

# CASE STUDY

# ARROW

When Wolfie Allen visited the Dogs Trust centre at Evesham, Arrow, a Bull Terrier/Stafford cross, bounded in and jumped straight onto her lap in her electric wheelchair. A week later, this 'lovable thug', as she affectionately calls him, came to live with her and he is now a fully trained Assistance Dog, helping Wolfie with many everyday chores, including opening doors, unloading the washing machine and fetching the post and her mobile phone.

'Arrow was in the Special Needs Department at the Dogs Trust centre. As soon as I saw him, I could visualise what he could become and I thought, "I'm special needs, too, and we'll make a good team". I knew that we were going to be a great partnership when, a few days after he came to live with me, I dropped an orange on the floor. Arrow picked it up and gave it to me and after that he never looked back.

'At first he didn't know how to behave and used to jump up a lot but, with professional help, we socialised him and improved his behaviour, and now he's very careful with me. He knows that I'm different from other people and he's very

| | |
|---:|:---|
| **Age** | 4 years old |
| **Breed** | Bull crossbreed |
| **Size** | Medium |
| **Colour** | Tan |
| **Adopted** | Wolfie |

protective of me. Like all Bull Terriers, he's very stubborn but fiercely loyal. I understand him and use my body posture, facial cues and language to show him I'm boss and prevent him becoming over dominant.

'We've taught Arrow to perform a range of tasks, and when he's wearing his special coat and working, he puffs out his chest and is really proud of what he does for me. However, when we remove his coat and he's off duty, he knows that he's stopped working and becomes a soppy family pet and just relaxes and plays with us.

'The Dogs Trust staff were just wonderful. Before Arrow came home with us, they socialised him with people in wheelchairs, so he could be rehomed successfully.'

> **'They say that a dog is man's best friend, and Arrow really is mine! He gave me the confidence to get out of the house and, thanks to him, I've much more freedom.'**

# CHAPTER 7

# KEEPING YOUR DOG HEALTHY

We all want to do our best for our dogs and that means keeping them fit and healthy. You need to provide a nutritious, well-balanced diet and plenty of exercise and games as well as a set routine and security. All these factors contribute to your dog's mental and physical wellbeing. Your dog relies on you for everything, and it's so easy to give him what he needs and help him to stay healthy, contented and youthful.

# GUIDE TO GOOD HEALTH

It's relatively easy to know if your dog is mentally happy – he will be friendly, wag his tail a lot, and eat and sleep well. He will walk cheerfully beside you on a lead and won't be nervous or aggressive. If this is true of your dog, you're a responsible owner and you've done a really good job. However, how do you spot the tell-tale signs of illness or poor physical health and what should you look for in a healthy dog? You can use your regular grooming sessions to check your dog for any clues to current or future potential health problems.

## Body

The body should be well-muscled and not too fat nor too thin.

## Anal region

This should be clean and the dog should not lick it excessively or scoot his bottom along the ground.

## Claws

These should be level with the pads and not too long or curling back under his feet. They should not be broken and he should not limp.

## Ears

The dog should not shake his head or scratch at his ears. The insides should be pink and healthy looking and smell pleasant without visible wax.

## Eyes

The eyes should be clear and shiny and you should be able to see your reflection in them. Cloudy (or milky) looking eyes may need to be checked by a vet. There should not be any discharge or tear stains.

## Nose

This should be cold and damp with no discharge. It should not be cracked or sore.

## Teeth

These should be smooth and white – not yellow or chipped. The gums should look pink and healthy (not bleeding) and the breath should not smell unpleasant.

## Coat

The coat should be soft to the touch and he should not display any signs of chewing or scratching at his fur. It should smell pleasant and when you part the hairs, there should be no bald or sore patches underneath or sooty flecks that indicate fleas.

**Health checklist**

- Your dog should have a healthy appetite. He should eat his meals and show an interest in food.
- He should be eager to go out for walks and walk normally beside you without any signs of lameness or breathlessness.
- A healthy dog wants to play; showing him his favourite toy should make him excited.

# CHECK YOUR DOG'S HEALTH

There are lots of checks that you can do yourself at home to ensure that your dog is fit and healthy and to prevent many common health problems developing. When you're grooming him or relaxing quietly together in the evening, just carry out a quick health check to make sure that everything is OK.

## Nose

The warm nose, cold nose theory is largely a myth. Your dog's nose should ideally be wet and shiny and free of any discharge. Throughout the day, your dog's nose can be hot, cold, moist or dry but if it's prolonged, or if it's dry and cracked, you should make an appointment to see your vet. Rubbing a little petroleum jelly into a cracked nose can help to soothe and heal it.

## Eyes

Check your dog's eyes regularly – they should be clear and free of discharge. Some dogs do 'cry' tears naturally, and tears can stain, but most normal dogs should have clear, bright eyes, which do not water persistently. If the fur below the eyes becomes stained or matted, you can wipe it gently with some damp cotton wool and then pat dry. If you are worried, ask your vet for advice.

## Ears

Healthy ears should be clear of discharge and unpleasant odour. Some dogs have hair in their ear canals and may need more ear care than others. You can remove surface wax with twists of cotton wool. When checking the ears, look out for grass seeds and mites, especially in long-eared dogs like Spaniels. These need to be treated by the vet.

## Teeth

Your dog's teeth should be free of any plaque and tartar, and the gums should look healthy and pink. Conditions such as bad breath, bleeding gums, trouble eating, or pain in the mouth should be referred to your vet. Some people give their dogs dental chews to help clean their teeth, or brush them with specially formulated dog toothpaste.

## Coat

The coat should be glossy and full – not dry, dull or thin. There should be no obvious evidence of parasites or any skin irritation. Check your dog's coat regularly for fleas, ticks and mites. Using regular flea and worming treatments will help to keep him healthy and free of unwelcome parasites.

## Weight

Obesity is becoming a big problem in dogs as well as in humans. Your dog should have a definable waist when viewed from above and you should be able to gently feel his ribs from the sides, although they should not be clearly visible. Your dog should be able to exercise gently without becoming tired or breathless. If you think that he is overweight, ask your vet for advice on feeding him a suitable diet and providing an exercise regime.

Take care not to cut into the 'quick'.

## Claws

Your dog's feet are very important and you must keep the claws short and trimmed. If you hear them clicking on the floor, then they're probably too long. Road-walking will help to keep them short. If you are worried about trimming them yourself, ask your vet to do it for you. You must be very careful not to cut the 'quick' or they will bleed a lot. Check between the toes to look for any foreign objects, redness or swelling.

# WHEN TO VISIT THE VET

There are some times when a visit to the vet is unavoidable but taking your dog there does not necessarily mean that he is ill – he may need a vaccination. There are lots of simple things that you can do yourself at home to avoid a trip to your local surgery; this makes it easier for your dog, too.

## Worming

Worms are parasites that live in your dog's intestine and bowel. Not only can they be harmful if left untreated, but they can also have a serious effect on humans and children who come into contact with the infected dog's faeces. There is a wide range of worm control tablets on the market. You can buy them from your vet, local pet store or even supermarkets. Puppies need to be wormed more often than adult dogs, but it's very important to worm both regularly – check with your vet about how often you should do this.

## Fleas

A dog with fleas will usually keep scratching and may also show signs of excessive self-grooming. To confirm the diagnosis, part the coat around the

head or tail areas and look for flea droppings (like black coal dust). Eliminating fleas is important, and there are many products you can administer at home to solve the problem. Ask your vet or pet store to advise on which medication to use, then follow the instructions carefully. If your dog has a full flea infestation, don't forget to treat his bedding and your carpets and furniture, too. Fleas are common and are nothing to be ashamed of, but do mention it to canine- and cat-owning friends to prevent any unnecessary contamination.

You can apply the flea treatment painlessly.

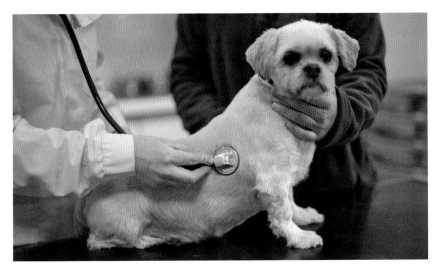

Get your dog accustomed to going to the vet for an annual check and booster jabs.

## Vaccinations

Puppies need to be vaccinated against the major canine diseases before being taken out in public places and meeting other dogs. Adult dogs should have annual booster injections to keep their immunisation up to date and to protect them from potentially fatal diseases.

## Neutering

Castrating or spaying is a routine operation to prevent unwanted pregnancies. Most rescue dogs will have already had this operation, which is considered sensible considering the amount of dogs left homeless each year. Make sure you check with the rescue centre that this is the case with your new pet.

## Insurance

Veterinary bills can be high if your dog needs an operation or has a long-term health problem, and pet insurance is a sensible option. It is not a legal requirement to have your dog insured, but it may save you money in the long run. Ask your vet for advice on choosing a policy.

**Make it fun**
We don't always enjoy visiting the doctor and it may be the same for your dog. If he is nervous about going to the vet, make it fun. Use praise and treats and let him know it's not all that bad.

# FIRST AID

Hopefully, first aid will be something you will never have to administer to your dog. However, accidents do happen, and it's always a good idea to have a well-stocked first aid box and a basic knowledge of what to do in an emergency.

## Bleeding

If your dog sustains an injury that causes bleeding, you need to quickly establish where the bleeding is coming from. Bleeding from an artery will have fast pumping, bright red blood; from a vein, it will be slower and less red. In either case, you must stop the bleeding quickly. Do this by applying pressure on the point of the bleed, using your hand or a clean cloth or towel. Keep the pressure on and talk calmly and reassuringly to your dog. In most cases, bleeding will stop within a couple of minutes. However, if you suspect that the bleeding is from an artery, then you must take your dog to the vet immediately. Take someone with you to keep the pressure on the wound.

## Choking

This can lead to suffocation and you need to act fast. It is usually caused when a piece of bone or splinter of wood lodges in a dog's throat. Rather than trying to remove it with your fingers (you may get bitten), ask someone to hold the dog and try to dislodge it with a spoon. If this does not work, hold the dog upside down, massage his throat and slap his back. You must seek veterinary help immediately if the object cannot be removed.

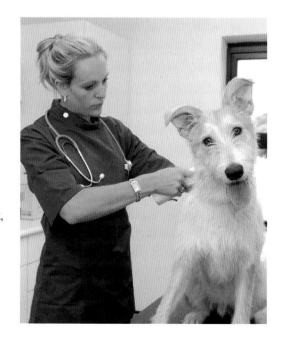

## Heat stroke

In either case, the affected dog will require urgent veterinary treatment. On the way to the vet, sponge him down with cool water, wrap him loosely in a wet towel and apply ice packs. As a responsible owner, this should never happen to your dog, and you should take care never to leave him in the heat or a hot car for any length of time – and always make sure he has access to water,

## Eye problems

Foreign bodies in the eye can be treated with human-type eye drops. Flood the eye so the object floats out. Eye injuries can be serious and will require urgent veterinary treatment.

## Fits and seizures

These can occur as a result of a high fever or as a reaction to an injury or illness. Follow the guidelines below.

- ➤ Keep your distance from the dog as he may bite you if he feels threatened or crowded.
- ➤ Move any potentially dangerous or harmful objects out of the affected dog's way.
- ➤ Ensuring that his environment is quiet, peaceful and dark may help to calm your dog, so turn off any external stimuli, such as the television, radio and bright lights. Contact your vet urgently for his professional advice.

**Canine first aid kit**
- ➤ Cotton gauze bandage
- ➤ First aid tape
- ➤ Plasters
- ➤ Cotton wool balls and tips
- ➤ Oral syringe (useful for getting water into a dog's mouth)
- ➤ Safety pins
- ➤ Tweezers
- ➤ Scissors
- ➤ Antibiotic ointment
- ➤ Antiseptic wipes
- ➤ Petroleum jelly

# YOUR SENIOR DOG

When you have an elderly dog, the best thing you can do is to make sure he is always comfortable. He's not going to act like a puppy and may not want to play fetching games, but he can still enjoy life to the full albeit at a slightly slower pace.

## Is your dog getting old?

A dog is usually considered a veteran after seven years of age. However, don't take this literally – there are plenty of 14-year-old dogs who are still tearing around. All dogs – like humans – age differently. Look out for some of the physical and mental symptoms of ageing, which are listed below.

## Physical changes

- **Overall slowing down:** you'll begin to notice slight changes when your dog gets up after lying down or tries to use the stairs. Many muscle, bone and joint conditions can be caused by arthritis and hypothyroidism.
- **Greying:** most old dogs begin to go grey around the face and muzzle, and this is much more noticeable in dogs with darker coloured heads.
- **Hearing problems:** whether your dog completely loses his hearing or just has the occasional problem, consult your vet to make sure that the deafness is caused by old age and nothing more serious.
- **Cloudy eyes:** older dogs tend to get a blue-transparent haze over the pupil. This may not affect their sight unduly unless cataracts are a concern in which case you need to take the dog to the vet – cataracts show as more of a white haze. In most cases, they can be treated.
- **Muscle wastage:** as dogs age, it's not uncommon for them to suffer some loss of muscle mass, usually around the hind legs.

## Mental changes

- **Less interest:** your dog may become less interested in his environment. He may not want to run or be so keen to go out for walks.
- **Sleep:** older dogs tend to spend much more time sleeping.
- **Cognitive dysfunction:** signs include disorientation, reduced interaction with people and other animals, sleep disturbances and incontinence. Affected dogs can be significantly helped by veterinary treatment.

# CARING FOR YOUR SENIOR DOG

As your dog gets older, you may have to modify and adjust his daily routine, diet and exercise to accommodate any health problems and make his life easier and more comfortable.

## Diet

Senior dogs may not need as much food as they age nor eat it with the same enthusiasm. If this is the case for your dog, don't worry unduly – it's perfectly normal. If you feed your dog a dry food, try adding a little water, gravy or milk to make it easier to chew. Give him smaller portions and if he doesn't finish a meal in one session, just leave it down for him to nibble at.

If you are concerned about his loss of appetite, treat him to tuna chunks or chopped roast chicken. However, watch out for any weight gain. Just like humans, some older dogs put on weight as they adopt a more sedentary lifestyle, and obesity can cause a range of diseases and shorten his life.

Your dog's appetite may diminish as he gets older; don't worry if this is the case.

## Exercise

Your dog will still enjoy a walk, but don't take him for three-mile hikes – little and often is better – and let him be the guide as to when he has had enough. He may well be just as happy with a potter around the garden. If he still enjoys a good run, let him do so, but be aware that he will most certainly tire more easily and may not want to chase a ball for half an hour.

## Home comforts

Make sure your dog's bedding is soft and thick, and that his water bowl is always at hand. Keep his bed away from draughts or anywhere too warm – extremes of cold or heat may make him uncomfortable. Occasionally, older dogs have the odd 'accident', so you may want to put some newspaper down near his bed – just in case. Remember to let him out more frequently, too.

## Grooming

Continue with your dog's usual grooming routine as he will enjoy this just as much as he ever did. Grooming will not only give you both time to enjoy extra closeness but will also help keep his coat in good condition, prevent dry skin and alert you to any unusual lumps or bumps which may need checking out by the vet.

## Treat him the same

To the best of his – and your – abilities, continue with all the activities your dog loved when he was younger. Make time to give him as much attention and affection as you possibly can. He is the same dog you brought home, and his love for you will not lessen as time passes.

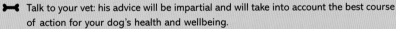

**Time to let go**

Putting your dog down is one of the hardest decisions you will make – he is part of your family. However, his life is based on fun, and if that is replaced by suffering, it's one of the kindest decisions you will make.

- Talk to your vet: his advice will be impartial and will take into account the best course of action for your dog's health and wellbeing.
- Don't be scared: euthanasia is a very quick, peaceful and pain-free process. Your vet will give your dog an injection that will stop his heart. You will be able to stay with him throughout if you wish.
- Grieve: don't be ashamed of your feelings after losing your dog. Talk to people about it and cry buckets if you want to. Losing a dog is a very painful process, but it's important to remember the good times, too.

# USEFUL INFORMATION

## Rescue organisations

**Dogs Trust**
17 Wakley Street
London EC1V 7RQ
Tel: 020 7837 0006
www.dogstrust.org.uk

**Animal Samaritans**
PO Box 154
Bexleyheath
Kent DA16 2WS
Tel: 020 8303 1859
www.animalsamaritans.org.uk

**Battersea Dogs' Home**
4 Battersea Park Road
London SW8 4AA
Tel: 020 7622 3626
www.dogshome.org

**Blue Cross**
Shilton Road
Burford
Oxon OX18 4PF
Tel: 01993 822651
www.bluecross.org.uk

**National Animal Welfare Trust**
Tyler's Way
Watford
Hertfordshire WD25 8WT
Tel: 020 8950 0177
www.nawt.org.uk

**RSPCA**
Wilberforce Way
Southwater
Horsham
West Sussex RH13 9RS
Tel: 0300 12344 555
www.rspca.org.uk

**Wood Green Animal Shelters**
601 Lordship Lane
Wood Green
London N22 5LG
Tel: 0844 248 8181
www.woodgreen.org.uk

**Wood Green Animal Shelters (Cambridge)**
King's Bush Farm
London Road
Godmanchester
Cambridgeshire PE29 2NH
Tel: 0844 248 8181
www.woodgreen.org.uk

**Wood Green Animal Shelters (Heydon)**
Highway Cottage
Heydon
Herts SG8 8PN
Tel: 0844 248 8181
www.woodgreen.org.uk

**Other rescue organisations**
www.staffycross.org

www.oldies.org.uk
www.dogrescuenorfolk.com
www.dogsos.co.uk
www.hoperescue.org.uk
www.nasatrust.co.uk
www.keithsrescuedogs.org
www.mutts-in-distress.org.uk

# Useful organisations

## Animal Health Trust

Animal welfare charity focusing on health and providing genetic testing and specialist veterinary care.
Lanwades Park
Kentford
Newmarket
Suffolk CB8 7UU
Tel: 01638 751000
www.aht.org.uk

## Association of Pet Behaviour Counsellors

International network of qualified counsellors treating behaviour problems in pets.
PO Box 46
Worcester WR8 9YS
Tel: 01386 751151
Email: apbc@petbcent.demon.co.uk
www.apbc.org.uk

## Association of Pet Dog Trainers

PO Box 17
Kempsford
Gloucester GL7 4W2
Tel: 01285 810811
www.apdt.co.uk

## British Veterinary Association

7 Mansfield Street
London W1G 9NQ
Tel: 020 7636 6541
www.bva.co.uk

## Cinnamon Trust

Charity providing benefits to the wellbeing of elderly pet owners.
10 Market Square
Hayle
Cornwall TR27 4HE
Tel: 01736 757900
www.cinnamon.org.uk

## DEFRA

For full details on Pets Passports and the PETS Travel Scheme.
Tel: 08450 335677
Email: helpline@defra.gsi/gov.uk
www.defra.gov.uk

## The Kennel Club

1–5 Clarges Street
Piccadilly
London W1J 8AB
Tel: 0844 463 3980
www.thekennelclub.org.uk

## The Mayhew Animal Home

Provides advice, care and assistance to pet owners, plus rehabilitation and rehoming services.
Trenmar Gardens
Kensal Green
London NW10 6BJ
Tel: 0208 969 0178
www.mayhewanimalhome.org

**National Dog Tattoo Register**
For more information on tattooing.
www.dog-register.co.uk

**PDSA**
Provides health advice and free
veterinary services for pet owners
on low incomes.
PDSA House
Whitechapel Way
Priorslee
Telford
Shropshire TF2 9PQ
Tel: 01952 290999
www.pdsa.org.uk

**Pet Care Trust**
Charity promoting responsible pet
ownership.
Bedford Business Centre
170 Mile Road
Bedford MK42 9TW
Tel: 01234 273 933
www.petcare.org.uk

**Pet Health Care**
Online source of pet care
information.
2nd floor Parkside
Horsham
West Sussex RH12 1XA
www.pethealthcare.co.uk

**PetLog**
For more information on
microchipping and tattooing.
www.thekennelclub.org.uk/meet/petl
og.html

**Pets as Therapy (PAT)**
Charity providing therapeutic pet
visits to hospitals and residential
homes.
3a Grange Farm Cottages
Wycombe Road
Saunderton
Princes Risborough
Bucks HP27 9NS
Tel: 01844 345445
www.petsastherapy.org

**Puppy School**
PO Box 186
Chipping Norton
Oxon OX7 3XG
www.puppyschool.co.uk

**Royal College of Veterinary
Surgeons**
UK regulatory body of the veterinary
profession.
Belgravia House
62–64 Horseferry Road
London SW1P 2AF
Tel: 0207 222 2001
www.rcvs.org.uk

**UK Animal Rescuers**
Comprehensive guide to animal
welfare organisations, rescue centres
and rehoming.
www.animalrescuers.co.uk

**UK Registry of Canine
Behaviourists**
Referrals: 01535 635290
www.UKRCB.org

# INDEX